lonely planet



TOP EXPERIENCES • LOCAL LIFE

PAULA HARDY, PETER DRAGICEVICH,
DUNCAN GARWOOD

# Contents



Gondolas

RASTOS PHOTOGRAPHER/SHUTTERSTOCK ©

## Explore Venice 33



## COVID-19

We have re-checked every business in this book before publication to ensure that it is still open after the COVID-19 outbreak. However, the economic and social impacts of COVID-19 will continue to be felt long after the outbreak has been contained, and many businesses, services and events referenced in this guide may experience ongoing restrictions. Some businesses may be temporarily closed, have changed their opening hours and services, or require bookings; some unfortunately could have closed permanently. We suggest you check with venues before visiting for the latest information.

## Survival Guide 171



## Special Features

# Venice's Top Experiences

## Marvel at dome mosaics in Basilica di San Marco (p36)

S-F/SHUTTERSTOCK ©

JAVEN/SHUTTERSTOCK ©

## Indulge in history at Palazzo Ducale (p40)

PAVEL TVRDY/SHUTTERSTOCK ©

## Go Gothic at I Frari (p88)

TATYANA ABRAMOVICH/SHUTTERSTOCK ©

## Shop for fresh food at Rialto Market (p90)

## Visit the palatial Peggy Guggenheim Collection (p66)

EQROY/SHUTTERSTOCK ©

BALONCICI/SHUTTERSTOCK ©

Admire art at Gallerie dell'Accademia (p64)

## Tour Tintoretto at Scuola Grande di San Rocco (p86)

VVOE/SHUTTERSTOCK ©

## Experience the ages at Basilica di Santa Maria Assunta & Torcello (p154)

ALIAKSANDR ANTANOVICH/SHUTTERSTOCK ©

FAINA GUREVICH/SHUTTERSTOCK ©

**Explore Campo del Ghetto Nuovo & the Ghetto (p116)**

**Admire the view from Basilica di San Giorgio Maggiore (p152)**

V_E/SHUTTERSTOCK ©

# Dining Out

*The visual blitz that is Venice tends to leave visitors weak-kneed and grasping for the nearest panino (sandwich). But there's more to La Serenissima than simple carb-loading. For centuries Venice has gone beyond the call of dietary duty, and lavished visitors with inventive feasts. Now it's your turn to devour addictive cicheti (Venetian tapas) and a lagoon's worth of succulent seafood.*

## Venetian Cuisine

Cross-cultural fusion fare is old news here, dating back to Marco Polo's heyday. Thirteenth-century Venetian cookbooks include recipes for fish with galangal, saffron and ginger; a tradition that still inspires dishes at nosh spots like Bistrot de Venise (p53) and Osteria Trefanti (p102). Don't be surprised if some dishes taste vaguely Turkish or Greek, reflecting Venice's trading partners for over a millennium. Spice-route flavours can be savoured in signature Venetian recipes such as *sarde in saor,* traditionally made with sardines in a tangy onion marinade.

## Cicheti

*Cicheti* (pictured) are some of the best culinary finds in Italy, served at lunch and from around 6pm to 8pm. They range from basic bar snacks (spicy meatballs, fresh tomato and basil bruschetta) to highly inventive small plates. Prices start at €1 for tasty meatballs and range from €3 to €6 for gourmet fantasias.

## Best Classic Venetian

**Antiche Carampane** Excellent seafood and moreish *fritto misto* (fried seafood) in Venice's former red-light corner. (p102)

**Trattoria Altanella** Authentic Venetian recipes served up by the same family since 1920. (p165)

**Da Codroma** Venetian dishes accredited by Slow Food. (p77)

## Inventive Venetian

**Venissa** Graze on the island landscape in lagoon-inspired dishes by rising culinary talents. (p166)

**Ristorante Glam** A modern take on Venetian classics

PFIFFER/SHUTTERSTOCK ©

from a Michelin-starred chef. (p102)

**CoVino** A pocket-sized showcase for Slow Food produce. (p142)

**Estro** Gourmet *cicheti* and highly creative Venetian cooking. (p75)

## Best Cicheti

**All'Arco** Market-fresh morsels and zingy *prosecco* close to the Rialto Market. (p102)

**Vino Vero** Inventive bar snacks accompanied by natural-process wines. (p119)

**Dai Zemei** Unexpected, creative concoctions from food- and wine-obsessed twins. (p104)

## Best Waterfront Dining

**Trattoria Altanella** Wine, dine and sigh on a balcony that hovers right over the water. (p165)

**Riviera** Perfectly positioned on the Zattere for hot-pink sunsets and romance. (p74)

**La Palanca** Panoramic waterfront dining at mere-mortal prices. (p166)

## Best Cheap Eats

**All'Arco** Stand-up gourmet bites made with prime Rialto produce. (p102)

**Snack Bar Ai Nomboli** Inspired sandwiches with quality ingredients. (p104)

**Pasticceria Tonolo** Best pastry shop in Venice. (p76)

**Didovich** An all-day eatery with outstanding outdoor seating. (p143)

### Top Tips

If all that produce and tradition inspires the chef within, sign up for a Venetian cooking course. **Acquolina Cooking School** (p164) runs four- and eight-hour courses, the latter option including a morning trip to the Rialto Market. It also offers multiday courses, including accommodation.

# Bar Open

*When the siren sounds for acqua alta (high tide), Venetians close up shop and head home to put up their flood barriers – then pull on their boots and head right back out again. Why let floods disrupt a toast? It's not just a turn of phrase: come hell or high water, Venetians will find a way to have a good time.*

## What to Order

No rules seem to apply to drinking in Venice. No mixing spirits and wine? Venice's classic cocktails suggest otherwise; try a *spritz* (pictured), made with prosecco, soda water and bittersweet Aperol, bitter Campari or herbaceous Cynar. Price is not an indicator of quality – you can pay €2.50 for a respectable *spritz*, or live to regret that €16 Bellini tomorrow (ouch). If you're not pleased with your drink, leave it and move on to the next *bacaro*. Don't be shy about asking fellow drinkers what they recommend; happy hour is a highly sociable affair.

## DOC Versus IGT

In Italy, the official DOC *(denominazione d'origine controllata)* and elite DOCG (DOC *garantita* – guaranteed) designations are assurances of top-notch *vino*. Yet, successful as its wines are, the Veneto also bucks the DOC/DOCG system. Many of the region's small-production wineries can't be bothered with such external validation as they already sell out to Venetian bars and restaurants. As a result, some top producers prefer the IGT *(indicazione geografica tipica)* designation, which guarantees grapes typical of the region but leaves winemakers room to experiment.

## Best Wine Bars

**Vino Vero** Natural, biodynamic and boutique drops in a standout Cannaregio wine bar. (p119)

**Al Prosecco** A showcase of Italy's finest natural-process wines and biodynamic viticulture. (p105)

KOSTASTUDIO/SHUTTERSTOCK ©

**Ai Pugni** Nightly canalside crowds and a long, interesting, ever-changing choice of *vino* by the glass. (p79)

**Timon** Top-class wines by the glass and live music sets canalside. (p119)

**Enoteca Mascareta** Inspired wines by the glass, including the owner's very own organic *prosecco*. (p145)

## Best for Beer

**Birre da Tutto il Mondo o Quasi** Venice's top beer bar keeps punters purring with over 100 brews. (p129)

**La Cantina** House-brand beer Gaston is a winner with sud-loving locals. (p129)

**Il Santo Bevitore** Trappist ales, seasonal stouts and chat-igniting football matches on the TV. (p128)

## Best Signature Cocktails

**Harry's Bar** The driest classic in town is Harry's gin-heavy martini (no olive). (p57)

**Locanda Cipriani** Harry's famous white-peach bellini tastes even better at Cipriani's island retreat. (p165)

**Bar Longhi** Drink top-class cocktails like the orange martini in a jewel-like interior. (p57)

**Bar Terrazza Danieli** Apricot and orange moonlight with gin and grenadine in the Danieli. (p144)

## Best Cafes

**Caffè Florian** An 18th-century time-warp in show-off Piazza San Marco. (p45)

**Grancaffè Quadri** This baroque bar-cafe has been serving punters since 1699. (p57)

**Torrefazione Cannaregio** A veteran coffee roaster famed for its hazelnut-laced espresso. (p128)

**Caffè del Doge** A serious selection of world coffees, including the rare kopi luwak. (p106)

# Treasure Hunt

*Beyond the world-famous museums and architecture is Venice's best-kept secret: the shopping. No illustrious shopping career is complete without trolling Venice for one-of-a-kind, artisan-made finds. All those souvenir tees and kitschy masks are decoys for the amateurs. Dig deeper and you'll stumble across the prized stuff – genuine, local and nothing short of inspiring.*

## Studio Visits

For your travelling companions who aren't sold on shopping, here's a convincing argument: in Venice, it really is an educational experience. In backstreet artisans' studios, you can watch ancient techniques used to make strikingly modern *carta memorizzata* (marbled paper) and Murano glass (pictured). Studios cluster together, so to find unique pieces, just wander key artisan areas: San Polo around Calle Seconda dei Saoneri; Santa Croce around Campo Santa Maria Mater Domini; San Marco along Frezzeria and Calle de la Botteghe; Dorsoduro around the Peggy Guggenheim Collection; and Murano.

## Best Original Venice Souvenirs

**Pied à Terre** *Furlane* (gondolier shoes). (p95)

**Gianni Basso** Calling cards with the lion of San Marco. (p130)

**Paolo Brandolisio** Miniature *forcole* (carved gondola oarlocks). (p149)

**Gilberto Penzo** Scale-model gondolas. (p113)

## Best Venetian Home Decor

**Fortuny Tessuti Artistici** Luxury, handmade textiles from an Italian style icon. (p159)

**ElleElle** Fetching sets of affordable hand-blown glass. (p157)

**Chiarastella Cattana** Sophisticated linens to restyle every corner of your *palazzo.* (p59)

**Madera** Forward-thinking objects, from chopping blocks to floor lamps. (p81)

## Best Venetian Fashion

**L'Armadio di Coco Luxury Vintage** Couture fashions of yesteryear at affordable prices. (p59)

NEIRFY/SHUTTERSTOCK ©

**Venetia Studium** Delphos tunic dresses and hand-stamped silk-velvet purses. (p61)

**Venetian Dreams** Lagoon-inspired swirling necklaces made with antique seed beads. (p61)

**Emilio Ceccato** The official supplier of natty gondolier gear. (p113)

## Best Antiques

**Ballarin** A treasure chest packed with period furniture, lamps, glass and more. (p149)

**Antiquariato Claudia Canestrelli** A walk-in curiosity cabinet. (p81)

**Antichità al Ghetto** A nostalgic mix of Venetian maps, art and jewellery. (p131)

## Best Jewellery

**Oh My Blue** Cutting-edge creations from local and foreign designers. (p95)

**Marina e Susanna Sent** Striking, contemporary wearables good enough for MoMA. (p81)

## Best Leather Goods

**Atelier Segalin di Daniela Ghezzo** Custom-made shoes created with rare leather and seasoned style. (p60)

**Balducci Borse** Shoes and bags from a master leather craftsman. (p130)

**Kalimala** Natural tanning and top-shelf leather underlines goods for men and women. (p148)

Murra Embossed journals and leather satchels hand stamped with the Lion of St Mark.

# Show Time

*Since the fall of its shipping empire, Venice has lived by its wits. No one throws a party like Venice, from Carnevale masquerades to Regata Storica floating parades – plus live opera, baroque music and jazz year-round, and summer movie premieres and beach concerts.*

## Festivals

Venice has some of the most decadent and spectacular festivals in the world. Carnevale (pictured) brings partying masqueraders on to the streets for two weeks preceding Lent. Tickets to La Fenice's masked balls run up to €230, but there are costume displays in every campo (square) and a Grand Canal flotilla to mark the start. La Biennale di Venezia (Venice Biennale), the city's largest event, showcases architecture or contemporary art.

The Venice International Film Festival runs from the last weekend in August through the first week of September, bringing together international star power and Italian fashion.

Aside from the big-name festivals, Venice celebrates with November's Festa della Madonna della Salute and July's Festa del Redentore. Regatta season from May's Vogalonga (www.vogalonga.com) to September's Regata Storica (www.regatastoricavenezia.it) sees cheering crowds along canal banks.

## Live Music & Opera

A magnet for music fans for four centuries, Venice supplies a soundtrack of opera, classical music and jazz. You can still enjoy music as Venetians did centuries ago: La Fenice (p58) has been one of the world's top opera houses since 1792, while historical La Pietà (p148) orphanage is the original Vivaldi venue. Due to noise regulations in this small city with big echoes, shows typically end by 11pm.

MARIA TSYGANOVA/SHUTTERSTOCK ©

## Best Events

**Carnevale** Party in costume until wigs itch and livers twitch - about three weeks.

**Venice Biennale** Outlandish openings in pavilions tricked out like surreal doll-houses. (p140)

**Venice Jazz Festival** (www.venetojazz.co) Jazz greats and the odd pop star play historical venues, including Piazza San Marco, in July.

**Venice International Film Festival** (August to September; www.labiennale.org/it/cinema) Red carpets sizzle with star power, and deserving films actually win. (p140)

**Venice Glass Week** (www.theveniceglassweek.com) A week-long festival celebrating over a thousand years of artisanship in September.

## Best Live Music

**La Fenice** Divas hit new highs in this historical jewel-box theatre. (p58)

**Palazetto Bru Zane** Leading interpreters of Romantic music raise the Sebastiano Ricci–frescoed roof. (p108)

**Musica a Palazzo** Operatic dramas unfold in a Grand Canal palace, from receiving-room overtures to bedroom grand finales. (p45)

## Best Local Favourites

**Laboratorio Occupato Morion** A radical backdrop for rocking bands. (p147)

**Fondazione Giorgio Cini** Occasionally serves up top-notch, modern world music. (p163)

**Paradiso Perduto** Jazz, salsa and the odd legend in an arty, old-school tavern. (p129)

## Top Tips

- For upcoming openings, concerts, performances, festivals and events, check accredited ticket seller www.veneziaunica.com.
- During Carnevale book accommodation well in advance and avoid the San Marco area which becomes extremely crowded.

# Architecture

*From glittering Byzantine churches to post-modern palaces, Venice astonishes at every gondola turn. Its 1000-year architectural history has several high-water marks: pointy Venetian Gothic arches rounded off in the Renaissance; Palladio-revived rigorous classicism amid baroque flourishes; and stark modernism relaxing around decadent Lido Liberty (art nouveau).*

## Contemporary Venice

Despite the constraints of history, a surprising number of projects have turned Venice into a portfolio of contemporary architecture.

MIT-trained Italian architect Cino Zucchi kicked off the creative revival of Giudecca in 1995 with his conversion of 19th-century warehouses into art spaces and studio lofts. Since then London-based firm David Chipperfield Architects has breathed new life into the cemetery island of San Michele. Meanwhile, rebirth of the artistic kind underscores Fondazione Giorgio Cini's redevelopment into a global cultural centre. Across the canal Venice's historic Arsenale shipyards has seen its sheds turned into Biennale art galleries.

In addition, French art collector François Pinault hired Japanese architect Tadao Ando to repurpose Palazzo Grassi and the Punta della Dogana into settings for his contemporary-art collection, while Renzo Piano reinvented the Magazzini del Sale as a showcase for the Fondazione Vedova.

Culture and commerce co-exist in Dutch architect Rem Koolhaas' 2016 redevelopment of the Fondaco dei Tedeschi. Once a base for German merchants, the 16th-century *palazzo* now houses a department store and a publicly accessible rooftop.

## Best Divine Architecture

**Basilica di San Marco** Byzantine domes glimmer with golden mosaics. (p36)

**Basilica di Santa Maria della Salute** Longhena's bubble-domed marvel,

PEREKOTYPOLE/SHUTTERSTOCK ©

believed to have mystical curative powers. (p72)

**Basilica di San Giorgio Maggiore** Palladio's expansive, effortlessly uplifting church and cloisters. (p152)

**I Frari** A Gothic brick fancy with a scalloped roofline and a 14th-century *campanile* (bell tower). (p88)

**Chiesa di Santa Maria dei Miracoli** The Lombardos' little Renaissance miracle in polychrome marble. (p122)

**Schola Spagnola** The theatrical, elliptical women's gallery attributed to Longhena. (p117)

## Best Pleasure Palaces

**Ca' d'Oro** The grandest palace on the Grand Canal, with Gothic trilobate (three-lobed) arches and tiara-like crenellation. (p122)

**Palazzo Ducale** Don't be fooled by Antonio da Ponte's pretty pink Gothic loggia: this palace was the seat of Venetian power. (p40)

**Ca' Rezzonico** Renaissance grandeur gone baroque: designed by Longhena, finished by Massari and crowned with Tiepolo ceilings. (p72)

**Palazzo Grassi** Gae Aulenti and Tadao Ando peeled back rococo flourishes to reveal Giorgio Massari's neoclassical lines. (p50)

**Fondazione Querini Stampalia** Baroque beauty with high-modernist updates: Carlo Scarpa–designed gardens and gates, Mario Botta library and cafe. (p139)

## Best Modern Marvels

**Biennale Pavilions** High-modernist pavilion architecture, which often steals the show at Art Biennales. (p138)

**Punta della Dogana** Customs warehouses creatively repurposed into cutting-edge installation-art galleries by Tadao Ando. (p72)

**Negozio Olivetti** Forward-thinking Carlo Scarpa transformed a dusty souvenir shop into a high-tech showcase c 1958. (p53)

**Fondazione Giorgio Cini** Former naval academy rocks the boat as an avant-garde art gallery. (p163)

# Art

*Water may be the first thing you notice about Venice, but as you get closer, you'll discover that this city is saturated with art. Canals are just brief interruptions between artworks in this Unesco World Heritage Site, with more art treasures than any other city. Through censorship, plague and nonstop parties, Venice kept creating masterpieces.*

ARTONO/SHUTTERSTOCK ©

## Best Venetian Masterpieces

**Gallerie dell'Accademia** Veronese's triumph over censorship: *Feast in the House of Levi*. (p64)

**I Frari** Titian's Madonna altarpiece: *Assunta*. (p88)

**Scuola Grande di San Rocco** Tintoretto to the rescue: *St Mark in Glory*. (p86)

**Scuola Dalmata di San Giorgio degli Schiavoni** Home to Carpaccio's delightful cycle of paintings of Dalmatian saints George, Tryphone and Jerome. (pictured; p138)

**Basilica di Santa Maria Assunta** Byzantine craftsmen spell out the consequences of dodging biblical commandments in the *Last Judgment*. (p154)

## Best Modern Art Showcases

**La Biennale di Venezia** The world's most prestigious visual art showcase. (p140)

**Peggy Guggenheim Collection** Explore the defining collection of breakthrough modern artists. (p66)

**Fondazione Giorgio Cini** Peter Greenaway videos in Palladio cloisters and blockbuster shows in a naval academy. (p163)

**Punta della Dogana** Historical customs warehouses retrofitted for the future with installation art. (p72)

**Fondazione Vedova** Rotating exhibits powered by robots. (p74)

**Casa dei Tre Oci** Italian and international exhibitions of contemporary art and photography. (p159)

### Top Tips

- See more art for less: get the 16-church **Chorus Pass** (adult/student under 29 years €12/8) or the **Civic Museum Pass** (adult/reduced €24/18), which is valid for six months and covers single entry to 11 civic museums, including Palazzo Ducale, Ca' Rezzonico, Ca' Pesaro and the Museo Correr.

# LGBTIQ+

*Venice's LGBTIQ+ scene is low-key almost to the point of non-existence. There are very few queer-only venues and those that do exist are mostly on the mainland, in and around Mestre. That said, Venice is generally pretty gay-friendly and LGBTIQ+ travellers should feel welcome in most places.*

CLAUDIO DIVIZIA/SHUTTERSTOCK ©

## Best Events

**La Biennale** A showcase for European art and architecture, La Biennale has provided a platform for LGBT themes in recent years. (p140)

**Venice International Film Festival** The Queer Lion Award, won in 2021 by Gianluca Matarrese for his documentary *The Last Chapter*, is dedicated to films with a homosexual theme. (p140)

## Best Beaches

**Spiaggia degli Alberoni** At the southern end of the Lido, this gay-friendly strip was used as a location in Luchino Visconti's film *Death in Venice*.

**Spiaggia di San Nicolò** Another gay-friendly Lido beach, this popular *spiaggia* sits at the far north of the island.

### Top Tip

Gay venues often require membership of Arcigay, Italy's national LGBTIQ+ organisation. Membership cards cost €10 and are available at venues themselves or at **ArciGay Tralaltro** (☎049 876 24 58; www.tralaltro.it; Corso Garibaldi 41; 6-9.30pm under-30s only, 9-11am Tue) in Padua. Padua, an easy 40km from Venice, has an active LGBTIQ+ scene and offers a wider range of gay-friendly night spots than Venice.

# Museums

LUKEONTHEROAD/SHUTTERSTOCK ©

*Peek inside Grand Canal palaces donated to Venice, and you'll find they're packed to attic rafters with Prada couture, samurai armour and the odd dinosaur. Though he tried for 11 years, Napoleon couldn't steal all the treasures Venetians had hoarded for centuries. Generous benefactors have restored Venice's treasure-box museums.*

## Best Venetian Blockbusters

**Gallerie dell'Accademia** Watch Venetian painters set the world ablaze with saturated colour and censorship-defying art. (p64)

**Palazzo Ducale** The doge's home decor is the world's prettiest propaganda, featuring Veronese, Tintoretto, Tiepolo and Titian. (pictured above; p40)

**Museo Correr** Palace rooms dedicated to pink Bellinis and blood-red Carpaccios, plus philosophers by Veronese, Titian and Tintoretto in the library. (p50)

**Scuola Grande di San Rocco** Tintoretto upstages Veronese with action-packed scenes of angelic rescue squads. (p86)

**Ca' d'Oro** Baron Franchetti's treasure-box palace packed with masterpieces. (p122)

## Best Fashion-Forward Palaces

**Museo Fortuny** The radical fashion house that freed women from corsets keeps raising eyebrows. (p50)

**Fondazione Prada** Futurist suits, video art and Duchamp suitcases are making waves along the Grand Canal inside stately Renaissance palace Ca' Corner. (p98)

**Palazzo Mocenigo** Find fashion inspiration in this palace packed with Venetian glamour. (p98)

## Best Modern Art Museums

**Peggy Guggenheim Collection** Pollock, Rothko, Kandinsky and company make a splash on the Grand Canal. (p66)

**Palazzo Grassi** Murakami's manic daisies, Damien Hirst's shipwrecked treasures and other provocations in a Grand Canal palace. (p50)

**Ca' Pesaro** Klimts, Kandinskys and other modern masterpieces Venice slyly snapped up at the Biennale. (p98)

**Punta della Dogana** Mega-installations are docked inside Venice's ex-customs warehouses. (p72)

# Under the Radar Venice

MIRELLE/SHUTTERSTOCK ©

*Venice can sometimes feel like a city under siege as tourists flock to Piazza San Marco and the main Strada Nova thoroughfare. But know where to go and you'll discover it is possible to escape the crowds and find areas seemingly untouched by the hordes.*

## Best Quiet Neighbourhoods

**Castello** Escape to this, the quietest of Venice's *sestieri* to recharge your batteries and mix with the locals in the city's public park. (p133)

**Cannaregio** North of the busy Strada Nova, Cannaregio (pictured above; p115) intrigues with its casual bars and historic Jewish quarter.

**Giudecca** Across the Giudecca Canal from San Marco, this island is a favourite haunt of artists, and thanks to its lack of major sites remains relatively crowd-free. (p158)

**Torcello** The bucolic lagoon island of Torcello is well worth seeking out with its sheep and glorious 7th-century basilica. (p154)

## Best Under the Radar Sights

**Museo Fortuny** A stylish museum hosting creative exhibitions in the salons of art nouveau designer Mariano Fortuny. (p50)

**Basilica di Santa Maria Assunta** Sail out to Torcello to admire glittering mosaics at this 7th-century Byzantine-Romanesque basilica. (p154)

**Galleria Giorgio Franchetti alla Ca' d'Oro** Artistic treasures dazzle in one of the most beautiful buildings on the Grand Canal. (p122)

**Ca' Pesaro** Masterpieces of modern art star at this alternative to the vastly-more-popular Peggy Guggenheim Collection. (p98)

**Scala Contarini del Bovolo** Escape the San Marco crowds and enjoy rooftop views from atop this 26m-high staircase. (p52)

### Top Tip

Taking a tour is a great way of discovering Venice's shadows and secret corners. **Best Venice Guides** (p181) has a team of highly qualified guides who can tailor their tours to your specific interests.

# For Kids

MS VECTORPLUS/SHUTTERSTOCK ©

*Adults think Venice is for them; kids know better. This is where every fairy tale comes to life, where prisoners escape through the roof of a pink palace, Murano glass-blowers breathe life into pocket-sized sea dragons, and spellbound Pescaria fish balance on their tails as though spellbound.*

## Best Family Attractions

**Palazzo Ducale** Explore a Gothic prison on the Secret Itineraries tour. (p40)

**Torre dell'Orologio** Climb this clock tower for giddy views of the bell-chiming *automata.* (pictured above; p51)

**Museo di Storia Naturale di Venezia** Discover dinosaurs, mummies and adventures on the high seas. (p99)

**Lido Beaches** Sandy beaches and shallow waters make a perfect escape. (p160)

## Best Hands-On Learning

**Row Venice** Learn to row as gondoliers do. (p130)

**Ca' Macana** Be inspired and craft your own Carnevale mask. (p80)

**Acquolina Cooking School** Get to grips with strange lagoon creatures. (p164)

**Venice Italian School** Learn to order like a pro. (p105)

## Best Dining

**Caffè Florian** Hot chocolate in fairy-tale interiors. (p45)

**Rosticceria Gislon** Perennially popular roast chicken in a 1930s canteen. (p56)

**Serra dei Giardini** Napoleon's greenhouse is perfect for tea and cake. (p146)

**Osteria al Duomo** Great pizza in a walled garden on Murano. (p167)

**Suso** Top-notch gelato made from organic ingredients. (p55)

### Top Tip

Given the expense of eating out, many families find that opting for an apartment is a life saver. Not only will you have your own kitchen, but shopping at the Rialto is a memorable experience. **Views on Venice** (p172) have a good selection of family-friendly apartments to choose from.

# Island Escapes

*Drift away on the blue lagoon, and you never know where you'll end up next: at a fiery glass-blowing furnace, an organic farmers market at an island prison, an orphanage designed by Palladio. Venice's lagoon offers not only idyllic island retreats – beachclubs, vineyard lunches and farm-stays – but also outlandish escapes from reality.*

ANIBAL TREJO/SHUTTERSTOCK ©

## Best Destination Dining

**Venissa** Ultramodern, ultra-local seafood in an island vineyard. (p166)

**Acquastanca** Baked goods wedged between glass-blowing studios. (p165)

**Trattoria Altanella** Authentic Venetian in a vintage trattoria with a flower-hung balcony. (p165)

**Locanda Cipriani** A wood-beamed dining room and elegant silver service. (p165)

**Terra e Acqua** Fish risotto aboard a Venetian barge. (p165)

## Best Outdoor Attractions

Lido Beaches When temperatures rise, Venice races to the Lido to claim sandy beachfront.

**Torcello** Rare lagoon birds swoop lazily past the Byzantine *campanile* on this wild island. (p155)

**Venice Kayak** Explore the lagoon. (p165)

**Vogalonga** The regatta race is a fine excuse to laze around Mazzorbo, raising toasts to rowers' health. (p164)

**Fondazione Giorgio Cini** Explore the Borges Labyrinth behind Palladio's cloisters. (p163)

**JW Marriott Spa** Recline poolside at the Marriott's stunning rooftop spa with Venice at your feet. (p168

## Top Tips

- Outer islands are blissfully peaceful in the October–April low season, though some restaurants and shops close.
- Ask locals to point out favourite lagoon shorebirds, including white ibis, purple heron and cormorants.

# Four Perfect Days

## Day 1

BRIAN KINNEY/SHUTTERSTOCK ©

Begin your day on the Secret Itineraries tour of the **Palazzo Ducale** (p40), then break for espresso at **Grancaffè Quadri** (p57) before the Byzantine blitz of golden mosaics inside the **Basilica di San Marco** (pictured; p36). Browse boutique-lined backstreets to **Museo Fortuny** (p50), then pause atop Ponte dell'Accademia for Grand Canal photo ops, before the timeless drama inside **Gallerie dell'Accademia** (p64). Wander past **Squero di San Trovaso** then bask in the reflected glory of Palladio's **Il Redentore** (p159). Stop at tiny **Chiesa di San Sebastiano** (p72), before '*spritz* o'clock' in **Campo Santa Margherita**.

Finish at **Scuola Grande dei Carmini** (p73), the setting for costumed classical concerts.

## Day 2

CHRISTIAN VINCES/SHUTTERSTOCK ©

Start at the produce-packed **Rialto Market** (p90), sidestepping it to **Drogheria Mascari** (p111) for gourmet pantry fillers and regional wines. Visit Gothic show-off **I Frari** (p88) and its sunny Titian altarpiece then slip into **Scuola Grande di San Rocco** (p86) for prime-time-drama Tintorettos. Explore modern art at the **Peggy Guggenheim Collection** (p66), and contrast it with works that push contemporary buttons at **Punta della Dogana** (p72). Duck into Baldassare Longhena's domed **Basilica di Santa Maria della Salute** (p72) for blushing Titians. The hottest ticket during opera season is at **La Fenice** (p58), but classical-music fans shouldn't miss Vivaldi played with verve at **Interpreti Veneziani** (p45).

## Day 3

FRANKI1/SHUTTERSTOCK ©

Stroll Riva degli Schiavoni for views to Palladio's **Basilica di San Giorgio Maggiore** (p152). Seek out Castello's hidden wonder: **Chiesa di San Francesco della Vigna** (p138) or get stared down by statues atop **Ospedaletto** (p135) on your way to Gothic **Zanipolo** (p138). Dip into pretty, Renaissance **Chiesa di Santa Maria dei Miracoli** (pictured; p122), before wandering serene *fondamente* (canal banks) to reach **Chiesa della Madonna dell'Orto** (p122), the Gothic church Tintoretto pimped with masterpieces. Then tour the **Ghetto's synagogues** (p116) until Venice's happiest hours beckon across the bridge at **Timon** (p119). Finish with a romantic gondola ride through Cannaregio's long canals.

## Day 4

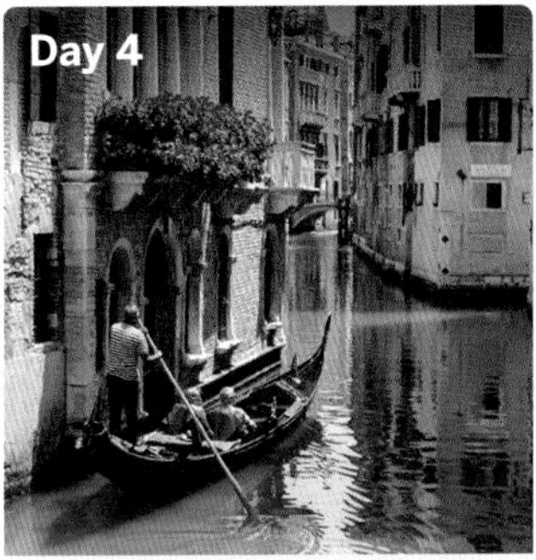

HELISSA GRUNDEMANN/SHUTTERSTOCK ©

Make your lagoon getaway on a *vaporetto* bound for Torcello for **Basilica di Santa Maria Assunta** (p154) and Burano to admire **Museo del Merletto** (p163). Take in the fiery passions of glass artisans at Murano's legendary *fornaci* (furnaces), and see their finest moments showcased at the fabulously renovated **Museo del Vetro** (p157). After Murano showrooms close, hop the *vaporetto* to Giudecca for some spa-loving at the **JW Marriott Spa** (p168) and unbeatable views of San Marco glittering across glassy waters.

Celebrate your triumphant tour of the lagoon with a *prosecco* toast and tango across Piazza San Marco at time-warped **Caffè Florian** (p45); repeat these last steps as necessary.

# Need to Know

For detailed information, see Survival Guide (p171)

### Currency
euro (€)

### Language
Italian, Venetian (dialect)

### Visas
Not required for EU citizens. Nationals of Australia, Brazil, Canada, Japan, New Zealand, UK and the USA do not need visas for visits of up to 90 days.

### Money
ATMs are widely available and credit cards accepted at most hotels, B&Bs and shops. To change money you'll need to present your ID.

### Mobile Phones
GSM and tri-band phones can be used in Italy with a local SIM card.

### Time
GMT/UTC plus one hour during winter; GMT/UTC plus two hours during summer daylight saving.

## Your Daily Budget

### Budget: Less than €120
Dorm bed: €35–60

*Cicheti* (bar snacks) at All'Arco: €5–15

*Spritz* (*prosecco* cocktail): €2.50–4

### Midrange: €120–250
B&B: €70–180

Civic Museum Pass: €24

Midrange dinner: €35–40

### Top End: More than €250
Boutique hotel: €200-plus

Gondola ride: €80

Top-end dinner: €50–60

## Useful Websites

**Lonely Planet** (www.lonelyplanet.com/venice) Expert travel advice.

**Venice Comune** (www.comune.venezia.it) City of Venice official site with essential info, including high-water alerts.

**VeneziaUnica** (www.veneziaunica.it) The main tourism portal with online ticketing for public transport and tourist cards.

## Advance Planning

**Two months before** Book high-season accommodation and tickets to La Fenice, Venice Film Festival premieres and Biennale openings.

**Three weeks before** Check special-event calendars at www.veneziadavivere.com, and reserve boat trips.

**One week before** Make restaurant reservations for a big night out; skip the queues by booking tickets to attractions, exhibitions and events online at www.veneziaunica.it.

## Arriving in Venice

Most people arrive in Venice by train, plane and, more controversially, cruise ship. There is a long-distance bus service to the city and it is also possible to drive to Venice.

**Marco Polo Airport** (flight information 041 260 92 60; www.veniceairport.it; Via Galileo Gallilei 30/1, Tessera) is Venice's main international airport and is located in Tessera, 12km east of Mestre. Inside the terminal you'll find ticket offices for water taxis and Alilaguna water bus transfers

Regional and international trains run frequently to Venice's **Santa Lucia train station** (www.veneziasantalucia.it; Fondamenta Santa Lucia), appearing on signs as Ferrovia within Venice.

## Getting Around

Walking is often the easiest way to get around Venice. Cars and bicycles can be used on the Lido.

### Vaporetto

These small passenger ferries are Venice's main public transport – note the line and direction of travel at the dock.

### Gondola

Not mere transport but an adventure – and the best way to slip into Venice's smaller canals.

### Water Taxi

The only door-to-door option, but fares are steep at €15 plus €2 per minute.

### Traghetto

Locals use this daytime public gondola service (€2) to cross the Grand Canal between bridges.

BURANO ISLAND /YURIY BIRYUKOV/SHUTTERSTOCK ©

# Venice Neighbourhoods

**San Polo & Santa Croce (p85)**
Shop for fresh market produce, rub shoulders with divine art and indulge in some of Venice's best culinary adventures.

**Dorsoduro & the Accademia (p63)**
Explore fine art and golden-age splendour, all with prime Grand Canal waterfront views and a dash of nightlife.

**San Marco & Palazzo Ducale (p35)**
Packed with attractions (and people), from the basilica to the Doges Palace, this is unmissable Venice.

**Cannaregio & the Ghetto (p115)**
Hop through Cannaregio's top *cicheti* bars and experience the absorbing contributions of the Venice Jewish community in the Ghetto.

Basilica di San Marco

Palazzo Ducale

**Castello (p133)**
Venice's largest neighbourhood covers seafaring history, Vivaldi venues and the city's favourite public gardens.

Basilica di San Giorgio Maggiore

**The Lagoon & the Islands (p151)**
The attractions of Venice's teal-blue lagoon and outlying islands range from celebrated glass centres and former Byzantine capitals to beach resorts and arty isles.

40

# Explore Venice



## Venice's Walking Tours



Colourful houses on Burano Island TIPWAM/SHUTTERSTOCK ©

# Explore
# San Marco & Palazzo Ducale

*So many world-class attractions are packed into San Marco, some visitors never leave – and others are reluctant to visit, fearing crowds. But why miss the pleasures of the Basilica di San Marco, Palazzo Ducale, Museo Correr and jewel-box La Fenice? Judge for yourself whether they earn their reputations – but don't stop there. The backstreets are packed with galleries, boutiques and bars.*

## The Short List

- ***Basilica di San Marco (p36)*** *Joining the chorus of gasps at Venice's showpiece cathedral.*
- ***Palazzo Ducale (p40)*** *Marvelling at the lavish state rooms and dingy prisons at this Gothic landmark.*
- ***La Fenice (p58)*** *Bellowing 'Brava!' for an encore at Venice's jewel-box opera house.*
- ***Museo Correr (p50)*** *Going face to face with philosophers painted by Veronese and Tintoretto.*
- ***Caffè Florian (p45)*** *Sipping sunset drinks at Venice's most revered cafe.*

## Getting There & Around

**Vaporetto** Line 1 serves stops on the Grand Canal; line 2 is faster and stops at Rialto, San Samuele and San Marco Giardinetti.

**Traghetto** A gondola ferry crosses the Grand Canal from Santa Maria del Giglio.

Follow yellow-signed shortcuts from Rialto through Marzarie to Piazza San Marco. It's often quicker than the vaporetto.

**San Marco & Palazzo Ducale Map on p48**

Palazzo Ducale (p40) TATIANA POPOVA/SHUTTERSTOCK ©

Top Experience

# Marvel at dome mosaics in Basilica di San Marco

*In a city packed with architectural wonders, nothing beats Basilica di San Marco for sheer spectacle and bombastic exuberance. In AD 828, wily Venetian merchants allegedly smuggled St Mark's corpse out of Egypt in a barrel of pork fat to avoid inspection by Muslim authorities. Venice built a basilica around its stolen saint in keeping with the city's own sense of supreme self-importance.*

MAP P48, G4

St Mark's Cathedral

041 270 83 11

www.basilicasanmarco.it

Piazza San Marco

admission free

9.30am-5pm Mon-Sat, 2-5pm Sun mid-Apr–Oct, to 4.30pm Sun Nov–Apr

San Marco

### Construction

Church authorities in Rome took a dim view of Venice's tendency to glorify itself and God in the same breath, but the city defiantly created a private chapel for their doge that outshone Venice's official cathedral (the Basilica di San Pietro in Castello) in every conceivable way. After the original St Mark's was burned down during an uprising, Venice rebuilt the basilica two more times (mislaying and rediscovering the saint's body along the way). The current incarnation was completed in 1094, reflecting the city's cosmopolitan image, with Byzantine domes, a Greek cross layout and walls clad in marbles looted from Syria, Egypt and Palestine.

### Facade

The front of the basilica ripples and crests like a wave, its five niched portals capped with shimmering mosaics and frothy stonework arches. It's especially resplendent just before sunset, when the sun's dying rays set the golden mosaics ablaze. Grand entrances are made through the central portal, under an ornate triple arch featuring Egyptian purple porphyry columns and intricate 13th- to 14th-century stone reliefs. The oldest mosaic on the facade, dating from 1270, is in the lunette above the far-left portal, depicting St Mark's stolen body arriving at the basilica. The theme is echoed in three of the other lunettes, including the 1660 mosaics above the second portal from the right, showing turbaned officials recoiling from the hamper of pork fat containing the sainted corpse.

### Dome Mosaics

Blinking is natural upon your first glimpse of the basilica's 8500 sq metres of glittering mosaics, many made with 24-carat gold leaf fused onto the back of the glass to represent divine light. Just inside the narthex (vestibule) glitter the basilica's oldest mosaics, **Apostles with the Madonna**, standing sentry by the main door for more than 950 years. The atrium's medieval

### ★ Top Tips

- There's no charge to enter the church and wander around the roped-off central circuit.
- Dress modestly (ie knees and shoulders covered) and leave large bags at the **Ateneo San Basso Left Luggage Office** (Piazza San Marco; max 1hr free; 9.30am-5pm; San Marco).
- Between April and October, reserve 'Skip the Line' access through the website (€3 per person; children under five free) and head directly into the central portal. Present your voucher at the entrance.
- The best chance of beating the crowds is to get here early and wait for the doors to open.

### ✕ Take a Break

Bask in the afterglow of the basilica's golden magnificence within the jewellery-box interior of Caffè Florian (p45).

**Dome of Genesis** depicts the separation of sky and water with surprisingly abstract motifs, anticipating modern art by 650 years.

Inside the church proper, three golden domes vie for your attention. The images are intended to be read from the altar end to the entry, so the **Cupola of the Prophets** shimmers above the main altar, while the **Last Judgment** is depicted in the vault above the entrance (and best seen from the museum). The dome nearest the door is the **Pentecost Cupola**, showing the Holy Spirit represented by a dove shooting tongues of flame onto the heads of the surrounding saints. In the central 13th-century **Ascension Cupola**, angels swirl around the central figure of Christ hovering among the stars. Scenes from St Mark's life unfold around the main altar, which houses the saint's simple stone **sarcophagus**.

### Pala d'Oro

Tucked behind the main **altar** (admission €2), this stupendous golden screen is studded with 2000 emeralds, amethysts, sapphires, rubies, pearls and other gemstones. But the most priceless treasures here are biblical figures in vibrant cloisonné, begun in Constantinople in 976 CE and elaborated by Venetian goldsmiths in 1209. The enamelled saints have wild, unkempt beards and wide eyes fixed on Jesus, who glances sideways at a studious St Mark as Mary throws up her hands

## Basilica di San Marco

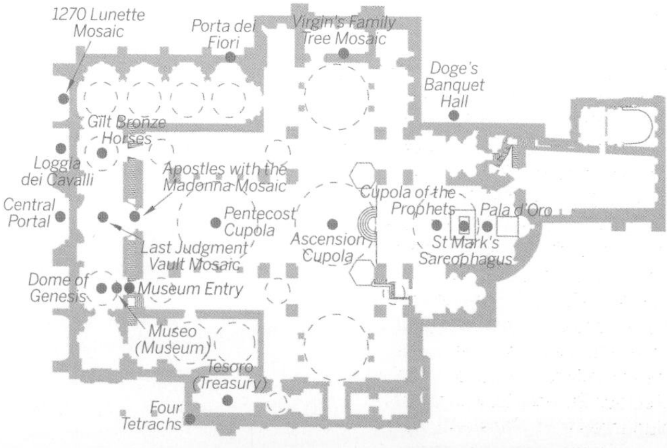

in wonder – an understandable reaction to such a captivating scene.

### Treasury

Holy bones and booty from the Crusades fill the **Tesoro** (admission €3), including a 4th-century rock-crystal lamp, a 10th-century rock-crystal ewer with winged feet made for Fatimid Caliph al-'Aziz-bi-llah, and an exquisite enamelled 10th-century Byzantine chalice. Don't miss the bejewelled 12th-century Archangel Michael icon, featuring tiny, feisty enamelled saints that look ready to break free of their golden setting and mount a miniature attack on evil. In a separate room, velvet-padded boxes preserve the remains of sainted doges alongside the usual assortment of credulity-challenging relics: St Roch's femur, the arm St George used to slay the dragon and even a lock of the Madonna's hair.

### Museum

Accessed by a narrow staircase leading up from the basilica's atrium, the **Museo di San Marco** (☎041 2730 8311; www.basilicasanmarco.it; Basilica di San Marco; adult/reduced €5/2.50; ⏰9.45am-4.45pm; ⛴San Marco) transports visitors to the level of the church's rear mosaics and out onto the **Loggia dei Cavalli**, the terrace above the main facade. The four magnificent bronze horses positioned here are actually reproductions of the precious 2nd-century originals, plundered from Constantinople's hippodrome, displayed inside.

Architecture buffs will revel in the beautifully rendered drawings and scale models of the basilica. In the displays of 13th- to 16th-century mosaic fragments, the Prophet Abraham is all ears and raised eyebrows, as though scandalised by Venetian gossip. A corridor leads into a section of the Palazzo Ducale containing the **doge's banquet hall**, where dignitaries wined and dined among lithe stucco figures of *Music*, *Poetry* and *Peace*.

Horses of St Mark

MEUNIERD/SHUTTERSTOCK ©

Top Experience

# Indulge in history at Palazzo Ducale

*Don't be fooled by its genteel Gothic elegance: behind that lacy pink-and-white patterned facade, the doge's palace shows serious muscle and a steely will to survive. The seat of Venice's government for more than seven centuries, this powerhouse stood the test of crashes and conspiracies – only to be outwitted by Casanova, the notorious seducer who escaped from the attic prison.*

MAP P48, H4

041 271 59 11

www.palazzoducale.visitmuve.it

Piazzetta San Marco 1

adult/reduced incl Museo Correr €25/13

8.30am-9pm Mon-Thu, to 11pm Fri & Sat Apr-Oct, 8.30am-7pm Nov-Mar

San Zaccaria

### Architecture

After fire gutted the original palace in 1577, Antonio da Ponte restored its Gothic grandeur. The white Istrian stone and Veronese pink marble palace caps a graceful colonnade with medieval capitals depicting key Venetian guilds.

### Courtyard

Entering through the colonnaded courtyard you'll spot Sansovino's brawny statues of *Apollo* and *Neptune* flanking Antonio Rizzo's **Scala dei Giganti** (Giants' Staircase). Recent restorations have preserved charming cherubim propping up the pillars, though slippery incised-marble steps remain off-limits. Just off the courtyard in the wing facing the square is the **Museo dell'Opera**, displaying a collection of stone columns and capitals from previous incarnations of the building.

### Doge's Apartments

The doge's suite of private rooms take up a large chunk of the 1st floor above the loggia. This space is now used for temporary art exhibitions, which are ticketed separately (around €10 extra). The doge lived like a prisoner in his gilded suite in the palace, which he could not leave without permission. Still, consider the real estate: a terrace garden with private entry to the basilica, and a dozen salons with splendidly restored marble fireplaces carved by Tullio and Antonio Lombardo. The most intriguing room is the **Sala dello Scudo** (Shield Room), covered with world maps that reveal the extent of Venetian power (and the limits of its cartographers) c 1483 and 1762.

### Sala delle Quattro Porte

From the loggia level, head to the top of Sansovino's 24-carat gilt stuccowork **Scala d'Oro** (Golden Staircase) and emerge into rooms covered with gorgeous propaganda. In Palladio-designed **Sala delle Quattro Porte** (Hall of the Four Doors), ambassadors awaited ducal

### ★ Top Tips

- Book tickets online in advance to avoid queues.
- Tickets (valid for three months) include Museo Correr (p50) but it's worth paying an extra €5 for a Museum Pass, which gives access to several other high-profile civic museums.
- Last admission is one hour prior to closing.
- Don't leave your run until too late in the day, as some parts of the palace, such as the prisons, may close early.
- Get here when the doors open to avoid groups, which start arriving at around 9.30am to 10am.

### Take a Break

Call into the humble but excellent **Pasticceria da Bonifacio** (041 522 75 07; Calle dei Albanesi 4237; pastries €1.10-2; 7.30am-6.30pm Fri-Wed; San Zaccaria) for a coffee, pastry or *spritz*.

audiences under a lavish display of Venice's virtues by Giovanni Cambi. Other convincing shows of Venetian superiority include Titian's 1576 *Doge Antonio Grimani Kneeling Before Faith* amid approving cherubim and Tiepolo's 1740s *Venice Receiving Gifts of the Sea from Neptune*.

### Anticollegio

Delegations waited in the **Anticollegio** (Council Antechamber), where Tintoretto drew parallels between Roman gods and Venetian government: *Mercury and the Three Graces* reward Venice's industriousness with beauty, and *Minerva Dismissing Mars* is a Venetian triumph of savvy over brute force. The recently restored ceiling is Veronese's 1577 *Venice Distributing Honours*, while on the walls is a vivid reminder of diplomatic behaviour to avoid: Veronese's *Rape of Europe*.

### Collegio & Sala del Senato

Few were granted an audience in the Palladio-designed **Collegio** (Council Chamber), where Veronese's 1575–78 *Virtues of the Republic* ceiling shows Venice as a bewitching blonde waving her sceptre like a wand over Justice and Peace. Father-son team Jacopo and Domenico Tintoretto attempt similar flattery, showing Venice keeping company with Apollo, Mars and Mercury in their *Triumph of Venice* ceiling for the **Sala del Senato** (Senate Chamber).

### Sala Consiglio dei Dieci

Government cover-ups were never so appealing as in the **Sala Consiglio dei Dieci** (Chamber of the Council of Ten), where Venice's star chamber plotted under Veronese's *Juno Bestowing her Gifts on Venice*, a glowing goddess strewing gold ducats. Over the slot where anonymous treason accusations were slipped into the **Sala della Bussola** (Compass Room) is his *St Mark in Glory* ceiling.

### Sala del Maggior Consiglio

The grandest room on the 1st floor is the cavernous 1419 **Sala del Maggior Consiglio** (Grand Council Chamber). The doge's throne once stood in front of the staggering 22m-by-7m *Paradise* backdrop (by Tintoretto's son, Domenico) where heaven is crammed with 500 prominent Venetians, including several Tintoretto patrons. Veronese's political posturing is more elegant in his oval *Apotheosis of Venice* ceiling.

### Secret Itineraries Tours

Further rooms can be visited on this fascinating 75-minute **tour** (☎041 4273 0892; adult/reduced €20/14; ⏱tours in English 9.55am, 10.45am & 11.35am). It takes in the cells known as **Pozzi** (wells) and the unadorned **Council of Ten Secret Headquarters**. Beyond this ominous office suite, the **Chancellery** is lined with drawers of top-secret files, including reports by Venice's far-reaching spy network. The accused might be led to the windowless **Torture Chamber**. Upstairs lie the **Piombi** (Leads), the attic prison where Casanova was held in 1756. As described in his memoirs, he made an ingenious escape through the roof. He would later return to Venice, enlisted as a spy for the Council of Ten.

## Palazzo Ducale

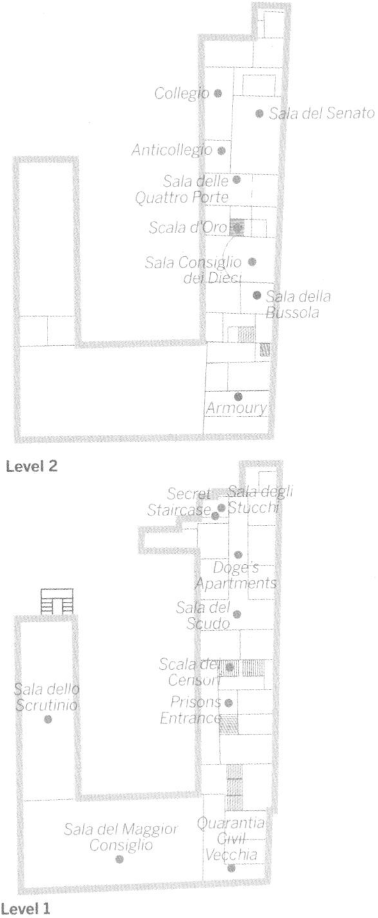
Collegio
Sala del Senato
Anticollegio
Sala delle Quattro Porte
Scala d'Oro
Sala Consiglio dei Dieci
Sala della Bussola
Armoury
Level 2
Secret Staircase
Sala degli Stucchi
Doge's Apartments
Sala del Scudo
Scala dei Censori
Prisons Entrance
Sala dello Scrutinio
Sala del Maggior Consiglio
Quarantia Civil Vecchia
Level 1

Walking Tour

# Music in San Marco

*Once Venice's dominion over the high seas ended, it discovered the power of high Cs, hiring as San Marco choirmaster Claudio Monteverdi, the father of modern opera, and bringing on baroque with Antonio Vivaldi. Today, music apps still can't compare to Venice's live-music offerings. While Teatro La Fenice is the obvious draw for opera lovers, try these other music destinations to immerse yourself in a Venetian soundtrack.*

**Start** Caffè Lavena; vaporetto San Marco

**Finish** Chiesa San Vidal; vaporetto Accademia

**Length** 1.5km; ¾ hour

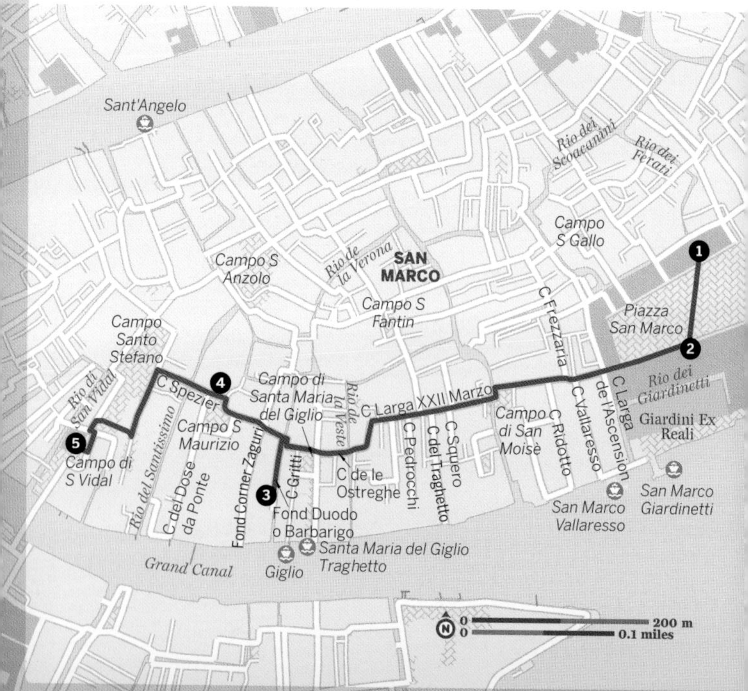

## ❶ Tarantella at Caffè Lavena

Opera composer Richard Wagner had the right idea: when Venice leaves you weak in the knees, get a pick-me-up at **Lavena** (041 522 40 70; www.lavena.it; Piazza San Marco 133/134; 9.30am-11pm; San Marco). An espresso at Lavena's mirrored bar is a baroque bargain – try to ignore the politically incorrect antique 'Moor's head' chandeliers. Spring for piazza seating to savour *caffè corretto* (coffee 'corrected' with liquor) accompanied by Lavena's nimble violinists.

## ❷ Tango at Caffè Florian

**Caffè Florian** (041 520 56 41; www.caffeflorian.com; Piazza San Marco 57; 9am-midnight Apr-Oct, shorter hours in winter; San Marco) maintains rituals established c 1720: white-jacketed waiters serve cappuccino on silver trays, and the orchestra strikes up as sunsets illuminate San Marco's mosaics. Piazza seating during concerts costs €6 extra, but dreamy-eyed romantics hardly notice. Among Italy's first bars to welcome women and revolutionaries, Florian's radical-chic reputation persists with its art installations.

## ❸ Arias at Musica a Palazzo

Hang onto your *prosecco*: it's always high drama in the historic salons of **Musica a Palazzo** (340 9717272; www.musicapalazzo.com; Palazzo Barbarigo Minotto, Fondamenta Duodo o Barbarigo 2504; tickets incl beverage €85; from 8pm; Giglio). The beautiful Venetian baroque palace overlooking the Grand Canal provides a unique, intimate setting as the audience follows the action from hall to hall, surrounded by authentic artworks and furnishings.

## ❹ History at Museo della Musica

Housed in the restored neoclassical Chiesa di San Maurizio, **Museo della Musica** (041 241 18 40; www.museodellamusica.com; Campo San Maurizio 2603; admission free; 9.30am-7pm; Giglio) presents a collection of rare 17th- to 20th-century instruments, accompanied by informative panels on the life and times of Venice's Antonio Vivaldi. The museum is funded by Interpreti Veneziani.

## ❺ Baroque Bravado at Interpreti Veneziani

Everything you've heard of Vivaldi from weddings and mobile ringtones is proved fantastically wrong by **Interpreti Veneziani** (041 277 05 61; www.interpretiveneziani.com; Chiesa San Vidal, Campo di San Vidal 2862; adult/reduced €30/25; performances 8.30pm; Accademia), who play Vivaldi on 18th-century instruments as a soundtrack for living in this city of intrigue – you'll never listen to *The Four Seasons* again without hearing summer storms erupting over the lagoon, or snow-muffled footsteps hurrying over footbridges in winter's-night intrigues.

# Walking Tour

## San Marco Royal Tour

*Dukes and dignitaries had the run of San Marco for centuries, and now it's your turn on this royal tour that ends with your own palace intrigue.*

**Start** Piazzetta San Marco; vaporetto San Marco

**Finish** Scala Contarini del Bovolo; vaporetto Sant'Angelo

**Length** 2.5km; 1¼ hours

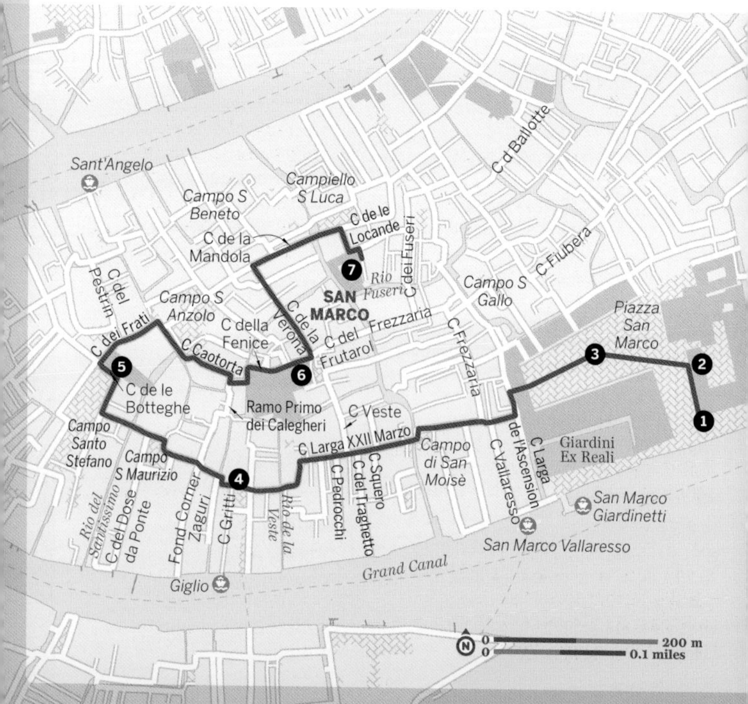

## ❶ Columns of San Marco

Venetians still hurry past these granite pillars, site of public executions for centuries.

## ❷ Palazzo Ducale

Pass by the **Ducal Palace** (p40) loggia, where punishments were once publicly announced before they were posted on the palace door.

## ❸ Piazza San Marco

In **Piazza San Marco** (San Marco), turn your back on the **Basilica di San Marco** (p36) to face Ala Napoleonica, the palace Napoleon brazenly razed San Geminiano church to build. Today it houses the entry to the **Museo Correr** (p50); the museum proper occupies the upper storeys of the Scamozzi-designed, Longhena-completed Procuratie Nuove. The right-hand arcade flanking the piazza is Mauro Codussi's 16th-century Procuratie Vecchie.

## ❹ Chiesa di Santa Maria del Giglio

Take Calle Larga XXII Marzo towards this baroque **church** (p52), sculpted with maps of Rome and five cities that were Venetian possessions at the time.

## ❺ Chiesa di Santo Stefano

Stop to admire Bartolomeo Bon's marble Gothic portals as you walk past **St Steven's Church** (p50), and then continue around to the Campo Sant'Anzolo and look back. The church's free-standing bell tower leans 2m, as though it's had one *spritz* too many.

## ❻ La Fenice

After pausing to take note of Venice's famous opera house, **La Fenice** (p58), take canyon-like Calle de la Verona into the shadows and continue on to Calle dei Assassini. Corpses were so frequently found here that in 1128, Venice banned the full beards assassins wore as disguises.

## ❼ Scala Contarini del Bovolo

Snogging in *campi* (squares) is such an established Venetian pastime it's surprising doges didn't tax it – but duck into Renaissance **Scala Contarini del Bovolo** (p52) courtyard for privacy.

### Take a Break

Charming staff dispense delicious *cicheti* (Venetian tapas) from a central horseshoe-shaped bar in upmarket little **Black-Jack** (p58).

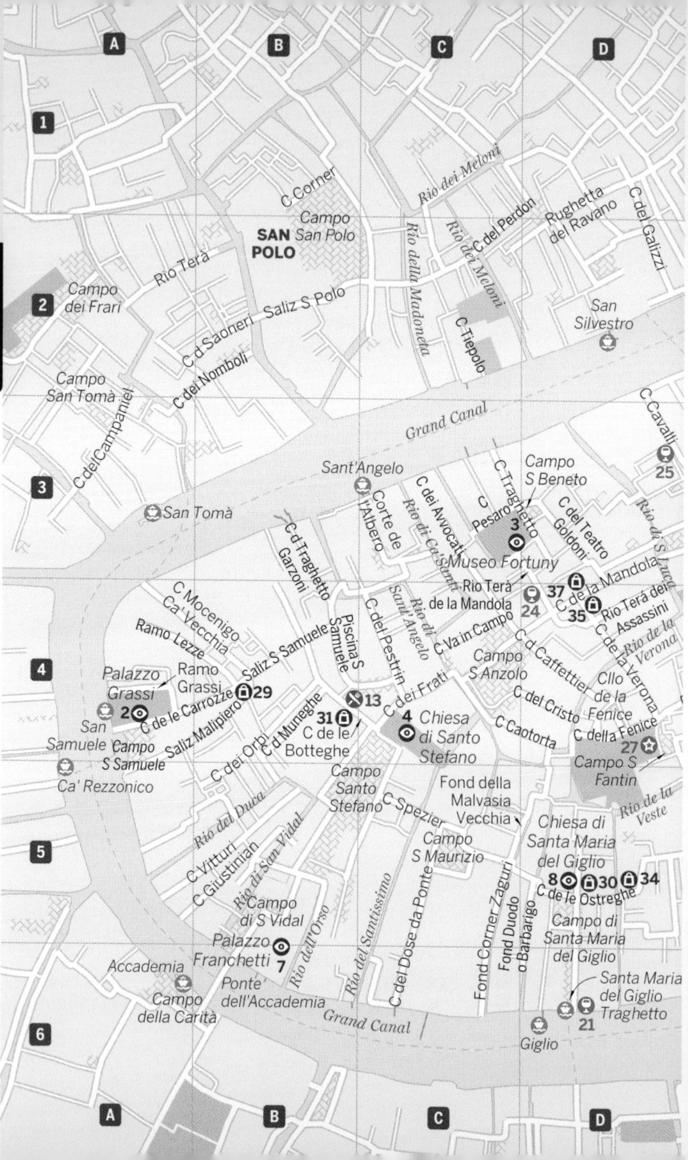
A
B
C
D
1
2
3
4
5
6
SAN POLO
Campo San Polo
C Corner
Rio dei Meloni
Rio della Madoneta
C del Perdon
Rughetta del Ravano
C del Galizzi
Rio Terà
Campo dei Frari
Saliz S Polo
C d Saoneri
C dei Nomboli
C Tiepolo
San Silvestro
Campo San Tomà
C del Campaniel
Grand Canal
Sant'Angelo
San Tomà
C Cavalli
25
Corte de l'Albero
C dei Avvocati
Rio di Ca' Michiel
C Pesaro
C Traghetto
Campo S Beneto
C del Teatro Goldoni
Rio di S Luca
3
Museo Fortuny
C d Traghetto Garzoni
Rio Terà de la Mandola
37
24
C de la Mandola
35
Rio Terà dei Assassini
C Mocenigo Ca' Vecchia
Ramo Lezze
Saliz S Samuele
Piscina S Samuele
C del Pestrin
Rio di Sant'Angelo
C Va in Campo
Campo S Anzolo
C d Caffettier
C de la Verona
Rio de la Verona
Palazzo Grassi
Ramo Grassi
29
C de le Carrozze
13
C dei Frati
Cllo de la Fenice
C del Cristo
2
San Samuele
Campo S Samuele
Saliz Malipiero
31
C de le Botteghe
C d Muneghe
C dei Orbi
4
Chiesa di Santo Stefano
C Caotorta
C della Fenice
27
Campo S Fantin
Ca' Rezzonico
Campo Santo Stefano
C Spezier
Fond della Malvasia Vecchia
Rio del Duca
Rio di San Vidal
C Vitturi
C Giustinian
Campo S Maurizio
Chiesa di Santa Maria del Giglio
Rio de la Veste
8
30
34
C de le Ostreghe
Campo di S Vidal
Palazzo Franchetti
7
Rio dell'Orso
Rio del Santissimo
C del Dose da Ponte
Fond Corner Zaguri
Fond Duodo o Barbarigo
Campo di Santa Maria del Giglio
Accademia
Campo della Carità
Ponte dell'Accademia
Grand Canal
Giglio
Santa Maria del Giglio Traghetto
21

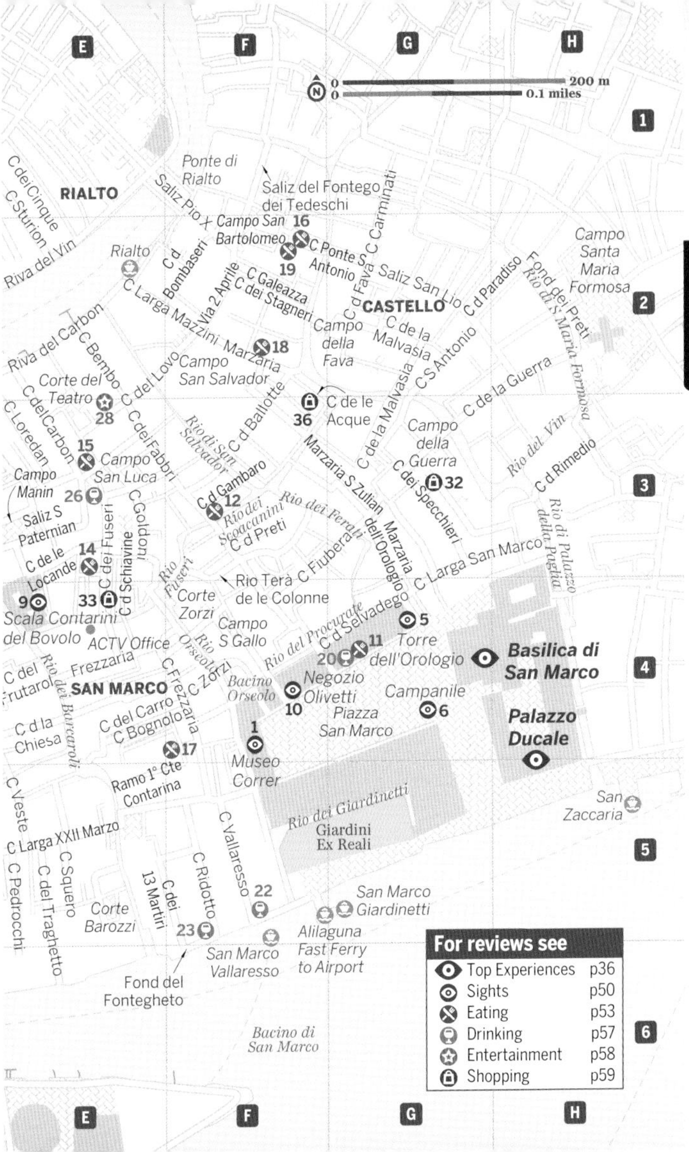
E
F
G
H
1
2
3
4
5
6
0 200 m
0 0.1 miles
RIALTO
CASTELLO
SAN MARCO
Ponte di Rialto
Saliz del Fontego dei Tedeschi
Saliz Pio X
Campo San Bartolomeo
C dei Cinque
C Sturion
Riva del Vin
Rialto
C d Bombaseri
Via 2 Aprile
C Galeazza
C dei Stagneri
C Larga Mazzini
Marzaria
C Ponte S Antonio
C d Fava
C Carminati
Saliz San Lio
C d Paradiso
Fond dei Preti
Rio di S Maria Formosa
Campo Santa Maria Formosa
Campo della Fava
C de la Malvasia
C S Antonio
Riva del Carbon
C Bembo
Corte del Teatro
C del Lovo
Campo San Salvador
C dei Fabbri
C del Carbon
C Loredan
Campo Manin
Campo San Luca
Saliz S Paternian
C de le Locande
C dei Fuseri
C d Schiavine
C Goldoni
Rio di San Salvador
C d Ballotte
C d Gambaro
Rio dei Scoacanini
C d Preti
Rio dei Ferali
C de le Acque
Marzaria S Zulian
C de la Malvasia
Campo della Guerra
C de la Guerra
C dei Specchieri
Rio del Vin
C d Rimedio
Rio di Palazzo della Paglia
Marzaria dell'Orologio
C Fiubera
C Larga San Marco
Rio Fuseri
Corte Zorzi
Rio Terà de le Colonne
Campo S Gallo
Rio del Procurate
C d Selvadego
Scala Contarini del Bovolo
ACTV Office
C del Frutarol
Rio dei Barcaroli
Frezzaria
Rio Orseolo
C Zorzi
C Frezzaria
Bacino Orseolo
Negozio Olivetti
Torre dell'Orologio
Basilica di San Marco
Campanile
Piazza San Marco
Palazzo Ducale
C d la Chiesa
C del Carro
C Bognolo
Museo Correr
Ramo 1° Cte Contarina
C Veste
C Larga XXII Marzo
Rio dei Giardinetti
Giardini Ex Reali
San Zaccaria
C Vallaresso
C Ridotto
C dei 13 Martiri
C Squero
C del Traghetto
C Pedrocchi
Corte Barozzi
San Marco Giardinetti
Alilaguna Fast Ferry to Airport
San Marco Vallaresso
Fond del Fontegheto
Bacino di San Marco
1
5
6
9
10
11
12
14
15
16
17
18
19
20
22
23
26
28
32
33
36
For reviews see
Top Experiences p36
Sights p50
Eating p53
Drinking p57
Entertainment p58
Shopping p59

# Sights

## Museo Correr MUSEUM

1 MAP P48, F4

Napoleon pulled down an ancient church to build his royal digs over Piazza San Marco, and then filled them with the riches of the doges while taking some of Venice's finest heirlooms to France as trophies. When he lost Venice to the Austrians, Empress Sissi remodelled the palace, adding ceiling frescoes, silk cladding and brocade curtains. It's now open to the public and full of many of Venice's reclaimed treasures, including ancient maps, statues, cameos and four centuries of artistic masterpieces. (041 240 52 11; www.correr.visitmuve.it; Piazza San Marco 52; adult/reduced incl Palazzo Ducale €20/13, with Museum Pass free; 10am-7pm Apr-Oct, to 5pm Nov-Mar; San Marco)

## Palazzo Grassi GALLERY

2 MAP P48, A4

Grand Canal gondola riders gasp at their first glimpse of the massive sculptures by contemporary artists docked in front of Giorgio Masari's neoclassical palace (built 1748–72). The provocative art collection of French billionaire François Pinault overflows Palazzo Grassi, while clever curation and shameless art-star name-dropping are the hallmarks of rotating temporary exhibits. Despite all this artistic glamour, it's Tadao Ando's creatively repurposed interior architecture that steals the show. (041 200 10 57; www.palazzograssi.it; Campo San Samuele 3231; adult/reduced incl Punta della Dogana €18/15; 10am-7pm Wed-Mon mid-Mar–Nov; San Samuele)

## Museo Fortuny MUSEUM

3 MAP P48, D3

Find design inspiration at the palatial home studio of art nouveau designer Mariano Fortuny y Madrazo (1871–1949), whose uncorseted Delphi-goddess frocks set the standard for bohemian chic. The 1st-floor salon walls are eclectic mood boards: Fortuny fashions and Isfahan tapestries, family portraits and artfully peeling plaster. Interesting temporary exhibitions spread from the basement to the attic, the best of which use the general ambience of grand decay to great effect. (041 520 09 95; www.fortuny.visitmuve.it; Campo San Beneto 3958; adult/reduced €10/8; 10am-6pm Wed-Mon; Sant'Angelo)

## Chiesa di Santo Stefano CHURCH

4 MAP P48, C4

The free-standing bell tower, visible from the square behind, leans disconcertingly, but this brick Gothic church has stood tall since the 13th century. Credit for shipshape splendour goes to Bartolomeo Bon for the marble entry portal and to Venetian shipbuilders, who constructed the vast wooden *carena di nave* (ship's keel) ceiling that resembles an upturned Noah's ark. (☎041 522 50 61; www.chorusvenezia.org; Campo Santo Stefano; museum €3, with Chorus Pass free; 🕑10.30am-4.30pm Mon-Sat, to 7pm Sun; ⛴Sant'Angelo)

## Torre dell'Orologio LANDMARK

5 ◉ MAP P48, G4

The two hardest-working men in Venice stand duty on a rooftop around the clock, and wear no pants. The 'Do Mori' (Two Moors) exposed to the elements atop the Torre dell'Orologio are made of bronze, and their bell-hammering mechanism runs like, well, clock-work. Below the Moors, Venice's gold-leafed 15th-century timepiece tracks lunar phases. Visits are by guided tour; bookings essential. (Clock Tower; ☎041 4273 0892; www.museicivicivenezianiit; Piazza San Marco; adult/reduced €12/7; 🕑tours in English 11am & noon Mon-Wed, 2pm & 3pm Thu-Sun; ⛴San Marco)

## Campanile TOWER

6 ◉ MAP P48, G4

Basilica di San Marco's 99m-tall bell tower has been rebuilt twice since its initial construction in AD 888. Galileo Galilei tested his telescope here in 1609 but modern-day visitors head to the top for 360-degree lagoon views and close encounters with the **Marangona**, the booming bronze bell that originally signalled the start and end of the working day for the *marangoni* (artisans) at the Arsenale shipyards. Today it rings twice a day, at noon and

Torre dell'Orologio clock tower

## See Venice like a Venetian

Throughout San Marco you'll be tripping over iPhone touting tourists. Everyone, it seems, wants to capture the perfect Venetian scene. Getty photojournalist and Venetian, Marco Secchi, will show you how during an in-depth **photo tour** (041 852 02 62; www.venicephototour.com; 2/3/5hr walking tours for up to 4 people €220/300/500) exploring the secret corners of the city. In particular, you'll learn how to capture the nuances of light and how to frame that masterpiece for the mantle. He can work with all types of camera, tailor tours to personal interests and arrange photography tours of the lagoon.

midnight. (www.basilicasanmarco.it; Piazza San Marco; adult/reduced €8/4; 8.30am-9pm mid-Apr-Sep, 9.30am-5.30pm Oct-Mar, shorter hours rest of year; San Marco)

## Palazzo Franchetti PALACE

7 MAP P48, B5

This 16th-century *palazzo* (mansion) passed through the hands of various Venetian families before Archduke Frederik of Austria snapped it up and set about modernising it. The Comte de Chambord (aka King Henry V of France in exile) continued the work, while the Franchetti family, who lived here after independence, restored its Gothic fairy-tale look and introduced a fantastical art nouveau staircase dripping with dragons. It's now used for art exhibitions, although the works have to compete with showstopping Murano chandeliers. (Istituto Veneto di Scienze Lettere ed Arti; 041 240 77 11; www.palazzofranchetti.it; Campo Santo Stefano 2842; 10am-6pm Mon-Fri; Accademia)

## Chiesa di Santa Maria del Giglio CHURCH

8 MAP P48, D5

Founded in the 9th century but almost completely rebuilt in the late 17th century, this church is distinguished by a series of six relief maps on its facade featuring Rome and five cities that were Venetian possessions at the time: Padua, the Croatian cities of Zadar and Split, and the Greek cities of Heraklion and Corfu. Inside are some intriguing masterpieces. (Santa Maria Zobenigo; www.chorusvenezia.org; Campo di Santa Maria del Giglio; €3, with Chorus Pass free; 10.30am-4.30pm Mon-Sat; Giglio)

## Scala Contarini del Bovolo NOTABLE BUILDING

9 MAP P48, E4

Under the Republic, only the Church and state were permitted to erect towers, as the structures could conceivably be used for military purposes. In around 1400 the Contarini family, eager to show off their wealth and power, cheekily built this non-tower instead. Combining Venetian Gothic, Byzantine and Renaissance elements, this romantic 'staircase' looks even higher than its 26m due to the simple trick of decreasing the height of the arches as it rises. (041 309 66 05; www.gioiellinascostidivenezia.com; Calle Contarini del Bovolo 4299; adult/reduced €7/6; 10am-6pm; Sant'Angelo)

### Negozio Olivetti ARCHITECTURE

10 MAP P48, F4

Like a revolver pulled from a petticoat, ultramodern Negozio Olivetti was an outright provocation when it first appeared under the frilly arcades of the Procuratie Vecchie in 1958. High-tech pioneer Olivetti commissioned Venetian architect Carlo Scarpa to transform a narrow, dim souvenir shop into a showcase for its sleek typewriters and 'computing machines' (several 1948–54 models are displayed). (Olivetti Store; 041 522 83 87; www.negoziolivetti.it; Piazza San Marco 101; adult/reduced €8/5; 10am-6.30pm Tue-Sun Feb-Dec; San Marco)

## Eating

### Ristorante Quadri ITALIAN €€€

11 MAP P48, G4

When it comes to Venetian glamour, nothing beats this historic Michelin-starred restaurant overlooking Piazza San Marco. A small swarm of servers greets you as you're shown to your table in a room decked out with silk damask, gilt, painted beams and Murano chandeliers. Dishes are precise and delicious, deftly incorporating Venetian touches into an inventive modern Italian menu. (041 522 21 05; www.alajmo.it; Piazza San Marco 121; meals €140-225; 12.30-2.30pm & 7.30-10.30pm Tue-Sun; San Marco)

### Bistrot de Venise VENETIAN €€€

12 MAP P48, F3

Indulge in some culinary time travel in the red-and-gilt dining room at this fine-dining bistro reviving the recipes of Renaissance chef Bartolomeo Scappi. Dine like a doge on braised duck with wild apple and onion pudding, or enjoy the Jewish recipe of goose, raisin and pine-nut pasta. Even the desserts are beguilingly exotic. (041 523 66 51; www.bistrotdevenise.com; Calle dei Fabbri 4685; meals €47-78; noon-3pm & 5pm-1am; ; Rialto)

### Trattoria Da Fiore VENETIAN €€€

13 MAP P48, C4

Rustic-chic decor sets the scene for excellent Venetian dishes composed of carefully selected seasonal ingredients from small Veneto producers. The restaurant is justly famous for its seafood dishes. Next door, the bar's *cicheti* counter serves tasty snacks at more democratic prices. (041 523 53 10; www.dafiore.it; Calle de le Botteghe 3461; meals €45-60; 12.30-2.30pm & 7.30-10.30pm; San Samuele)

## Keeping Venice Afloat

Impossible though it seems, Venetians built their home on 117 small islands connected by some 400 bridges over 150 canals. But if floating marble palaces boggle the mind, consider what's underneath them: an entire forest's worth of petrified wood pylons, rammed through silty *barene* (shoals) into the clay lagoon floor.

### High Tides

Venice is ingeniously constructed to contend with lagoon tides, so even a four-alarm *acqua alta* (exceptionally high tide) is rarely cause for panic. But on 4 November 1966, record floods poured into 16,000 Venetian homes in terrifying waves, and residents were stranded in the wreckage of 1400 years of civilisation. Thanks to Venice's international appeal, assistance poured in and Unesco coordinated 50 private organisations to redress the ravages of the flood.

Cleaning up after *acqua alta* is a tedious job for Venetians: pumping water out of flooded ground floors and preventing corrosion by scrubbing salt residue off surfaces. Venice's canals must also be regularly dredged, which involves pumping water out, removing pungent sludge, then patching brickwork by hand with a ticklish technique Venetians call *scuci-cuci*.

### Environmental Challenges

Venice and its lagoon are a Unesco World Heritage site – but in the wake of Tuscany's 2012 Costa Concordia shipwreck, Unesco expressed concern about the impact of cruise ships and unsustainable tourism. Locally, opposition to cruise ships was led by critics such as No Grandi Navi (No Big Ships), which spearheaded a successful campaign to have them banned from the lagoon. This eventually came in August 2021 when the Italian government barred vessels weighing more than 25,000 tonnes from entering the lagoon.

Meanwhile, responsible travellers are taking action – eating sustainably sourced, local food; conserving water; using products free of industrial chemicals; and above all, supporting local businesses – to help offset tourism impact, and keep Venice afloat.

## Ai Mercanti

ITALIAN **€€**

14 MAP P48, E3

With its pumpkin-coloured walls, gleaming golden fixtures and jet-black tables and chairs, Ai Mercanti effortlessly conjures up a romantic mood. No wonder diners whisper over glasses of wine selected from the vast list before tucking into modern bistro-style dishes. Although there's a focus on seafood and secondary cuts of meat, there are some wonderful vegetarian options as well. (041 523 82 69; www.aimercanti.it; Calle Fuseri 4346a; meals €35-40; 11.30am-3pm & 7-10pm Tue-Sat, 7-11pm Mon; Rialto)

### Marchini Time

BAKERY €

15 MAP P48, E3

Elbow your way through the morning crush to bag a warm croissant filled with runny apricot jam or melting Nutella. Everything here is freshly baked, which is why the crowd hangs around as croissants give way to focaccia, *pizzette* (mini pizzas) and generously stuffed *panini*. (041 241 30 87; www.marchinitime.it; Campo San Luca 4589; items €1.20-3.50; 7.30am-8.30pm; Rialto)

### Suso

GELATO €

16 MAP P48, F2

Suso's gelati are locally made and free of artificial colours. Indulge in rich, original seasonal flavours such as marscapone cream with fig sauce and walnuts. Gluten-free cones are available. (348 5646545; www.gelatovenezia.it; Calle de la Bissa 5453; scoops €1.60; 10am-midnight; Rialto)

### Osteria da Carla

VENETIAN €€

17 MAP P48, F4

Diners in the know duck into this hidden courtyard, less than 100m from Piazza San Marco, to snack

Baci in gondola, chocolate and meringue sweets

on *cicheti* (Venetian tapas) at the counter or to sit down to a romantic meal. The surroundings are at once modern and ancient, with exposed brick and interesting art. (☎041 523 78 55; www.osteriadacarla.it; Corte Contarina 1535a; meals €40-45; 9am-10.30pm Mon-Sat; San Marco)

## Rosa Salva

BAKERY €

18 MAP P48, F2

With just-baked strudel and reliable cappuccino, Rosa Salva has provided Venetians with fresh reasons to roll out of bed for more than a century. Cheerfully efficient women working the spotless counter supply gale-force espresso and turbo-loaded pistachio profiteroles to power you across 30 more bridges. Come lunchtime, the sweet pastries are replaced by plump sandwiches and hot deli plates. (☎041 521 05 44; www.rosasalva.it; Calle Fiubera 951; items €1.30-7.50; 8am-8pm; Rialto)

## Rosticceria Gislon

DELI €

19 MAP P48, F2

Serving San Marco workers since the 1930s, this no-frills *rosticceria* (roast-meat specialist) has an ultramarine canteen counter downstairs and a small eat-in restaurant upstairs. For a quick bite you'll find *arancini* (rice balls), deep-fried mozzarella balls, croquettes and fish fry-ups. No one said it was going to be healthy! (☎041 522 35 69; Calle de la Bissa 5424; meals €15-25; 9am-9.30pm Tue-Sun, to 3.30pm Mon; Rialto)

Caffè Florian (p45)

MAZUR TRAVEL/SHUTTERSTOCK ©

# Drinking

## Grancaffè Quadri

CAFE

20 MAP P48, G4

Powdered wigs seem appropriate inside this baroque bar-cafe that's been serving happy hours since 1638. During Carnevale, costumed Quadri revellers party like it's 1699 – despite prices shooting up to €15 for a *spritz*. Grab a seat on the piazza to watch the best show in town: the basilica's golden mosaics ablaze in the sunset. (041 522 21 05; www.alajmo.it; Piazza San Marco 121; 9am-midnight; San Marco)

## Bar Longhi

COCKTAIL BAR

21 MAP P48, D6

Gritti Palace's beautiful Bar Longhi may be pricey, but if you consider your surrounds – Fortuny fabrics, an intarsia marble bar, 18th-century mirrors and million-dollar Piero Longhi paintings – the price of a signature orange martini starts to seem reasonable. In summer you'll have to choose between the twinkling interior and a spectacular Grand Canal terrace. (041 79 47 81; www.hotelgrittipalacevenice.com; Campo di Santa Maria del Giglio 2467; 11am-1am; Giglio)

## Harry's Bar

BAR

22 MAP P48, F5

Aspiring auteurs hold court at tables well scuffed by Ernest Hemingway, Charlie Chaplin, Truman Capote and Orson Welles, enjoying the signature €21 Bellini (Giuseppe Cipriani's original 1948 recipe: white peach juice and prosecco) with a side of reflected glory. (041 528 57 77; www.cipriani.com; Calle Vallaresso 1323; 10.30am-11pm; San Marco)

### Coffee or Rent?

In San Marco the price of a sit-down coffee seems more like rent. Take your coffee standing at a bar like the locals do for €1 to €2.50. If you want to luxuriate inside the baroque cafes in Piazza San Marco, or idle in the outdoor seating, there's usually a €6 surcharge. Still, you do get to enjoy a top-class classical orchestra and one of the best views in the world.

## L'Ombra del Leoni

BAR

23 MAP P48, F5

Enjoy Palazzo Ca' Giustinian's peerless waterside Grand Canal position in this cafe-restaurant. Try to nab a seat on the outdoor terrace – it's the perfect spot to watch the gondolas come and go against a backdrop of basilicas. (041 521 87 11; Calle Ridotto 1364a; 9am-9pm; San Marco)

## Teamo

WINE BAR

24 MAP P48, D4

By day this is more of a cafe, but in the evening its little tables fill up with a mixed crowd, drinking wine and snacking on massive platters of *salumi* (cured meats) and cheese. (041 528 37 87; www.teamowinebar.com; Rio Terà de la Mandola 3795; 8.30am-10.30pm Fri-Wed; Sant'Angelo)

### Enoteca al Volto

WINE BAR

25 MAP P48, D3

Join the crowd working its way through the vast selection of *cicheti* in this historic wood-panelled bar that feels like the inside of a ship's hold. Lining the ceiling above the golden glow of the brass bar lanterns are hundreds of wine labels from just some of the bottles of regional wines that are cracked open every night. (041 522 89 45; http://enotecaalvolto.com; Calle Cavalli 4081; 10am-4pm & 6-10pm; Rialto)

### Black-Jack

WINE BAR

26 MAP P48, E3

Charming staff dispense delicious *cicheti* from a central horseshoe-shaped bar in this upmarket little place in the main shopping precinct. It's a great place for a snack and a tipple on your way to La Fenice or Teatro Goldoni; you could easily make a meal of it. (Campo San Luca 4267b; 7.30am-9pm; Rialto)

## Entertainment

### Teatro La Fenice

OPERA

27 MAP P48, D4

One of Italy's top opera houses, La Fenice stages a rich roster of opera, ballet and classical music. The main opera season runs from January to July and September to October. The cheapest seats (€15) are in the boxes at the top: the view is extremely restricted, but you will get to hear the music, watch the orchestra, soak up the atmosphere and people-watch. (041 78 66 54; www.teatrolafenice.it; Campo San Fantin 1965; tickets €15-380; Giglio)

### Teatro Goldoni

THEATRE

28 MAP P48, E2

Named after the city's great playwright, Carlo Goldoni, Venice's main theatre has an impressive dramatic range that runs from Goldoni's comedy to Shakespearean tragedy (mostly in Italian), plus ballets and concerts. Don't be fooled by the huge 20th-century bronze doors: this venerable theatre dates from 1622, and the jewel-box interior seats just 800. (041 240 20 14; www.teatrostabileveneto.it; Calle del Teatro 4650b; Rialto)

## Shopping

### Chiarastella Cattana HOMEWARES

29 MAP P48, B4

Transform any home with these locally woven, strikingly original Venetian linens. Whimsical cushions feature chubby purple rhinoceroses and grumpy scarlet elephants straight out of Pietro Longhi paintings, and hand-tasselled jacquard hand towels will dry your guests in style. Decorators and design aficionados should save an afternoon to consider dizzying woven-to-order napkin and curtain options. (041 522 43 69; www.chiarastellacattana.com; Salizada San Samuele 3216; 11am-1pm & 3-7pm Mon-Sat; San Samuele)

### L'Armadio di Coco Luxury Vintage VINTAGE

30 MAP P48, D5

Jam-packed with pre-loved designer treasures from yesteryear, this tiny shop is the place to come for classic Chanel dresses, exquisite cashmere coats and limited-edition Gucci shoulder bags. (041 241 32 14; www.larmadiodicoco.it; Campo di Santa Maria del Giglio 2516a; 10.30am-7pm; Giglio)

### L'Isola GLASS

31 MAP P48, C4

Backlit chalices and spotlit vases emit an otherworldly glow at this shrine to Murano modernist glass master Carlo Moretti. Strict shapes contain freeform swirls of orange and red, and glasses

Teatro La Fenice

etched with fish-scale patterns add wit and a wink to high-minded modernism. (☎041 523 19 73; www.lisola.com; Calle de le Botteghe 2970; ⏲10.30am-7.30pm Mon-Sat; ⛴San Samuele)

## Esperienze

GLASS

32 MAP P48, G3

When an Italian minimalist falls in love with a Murano glass-blower, the result is spare, spirited glass jewellery. Esperienze is a collaborative effort for husband-and-wife team Graziano and Sara: he breathes life into her designs, including matte-glass teardrop pendants and cracked-ice earrings. They also stock a range of women's clothing. (☎041 521 29 45; Calle dei Specchieri 473b; ⏲10am-noon & 3-7pm; ⛴San Marco)

## Atelier Segalin di Daniela Ghezzo

SHOES

33 MAP P48, E4

A gold chain pulled across this historic atelier doorway means Daniela is already consulting with a client, discussing rare leathers while taking foot measurements. Each pair of shoes is custom-made, so you'll never see your emerald ostrich-leather boots on another diva, or your dimpled manta-ray brogues on a rival mogul. Expect to pay around €1000 and wait six weeks for delivery. (☎041 522 21 15; www.danielaghezzo.it; Calle dei Fuseri 4365; ⏲10am-1pm & 3-7pm Mon-Fri, 10am-1pm Sat; ⛴San Marco)

Souvenir stalls on Ponte di Rialto (p91)

ROSTISLAV GLINSKY/SHUTTERSTOCK

## Venetia Studium

FASHION & ACCESSORIES

34 MAP P48, D5

Get that 'just got in from Monaco for my art opening' look beloved of cashed-up bohemians. The high-drama Delphos tunic dresses make anyone look like a high-maintenance modern dancer or heiress (Isadora Duncan and Peggy Guggenheim were both fans), and the hand-stamped silk-velvet bags are more arty than ostentatious. (041 523 69 53; www.venetiastudium.com; Calle de le Ostreghe 2427; 10.30am-7pm Mon-Sat, from 11am Sun; Giglio)

## Ottica Carraro

FASHION & ACCESSORIES

35 MAP P48, D4

Lost your sunglasses on the Lido? Never fear: Ottica Carraro can make you a custom pair within 24 hours, including the eye exam. The store has its own limited-edition 'Venice' line, ranging from cat-eye shades perfect for facing paparazzi to chunky wood-grain frames that could get you mistaken for an art critic at the Biennale. (041 520 42 58; www.otticacarraro.it; Calle de la Mandola 3706; 9.30am-1pm & 3-7.30pm Mon-Sat; Sant'Angelo)

## Camuffo

GLASS

36 MAP P48, F2

Kids, entomologists and glass collectors seek out Signor Camuffo in this cabinet of miniature natural wonders. Expect to find him wielding a blowtorch as he fuses metallic foils and molten glass into shimmering wings for the city's finest lamp-worked glass beetles and dragonflies. Between bugs, he'll chat about his work and sell you strands of Murano glass beads. (Calle de le Acque 4992; 10am-12.30pm & 1-5pm Mon-Sat; Rialto)

## Venetian Dreams

FASHION & ACCESSORIES

37 MAP P48, D3

High fashion meets *acqua alta* (high water) in Marisa Convento's aquatic accessories. La Fenice divas demand her freshwater-pearl-encrusted velvet handbags, while Biennale artistes snap up octopus-tentacle glass-bead necklaces. Between customers, Marisa can be glimpsed at her desk, painstakingly weaving coral-branch collars from antique Murano *conterie* (seed beads). To wow Carnevale crowds, ask about ordering a custom-made costume. (041 523 02 92; www.marisaconvento.it; Calle de la Mandola 3805a; 10.30am-7pm Mon-Sat; Sant'Angelo)

Explore

# Dorsoduro & the Accademia

*Dorsoduro covers prime Grand Canal waterfront with Ca' Rezzonico's golden-age splendour, the Peggy Guggenheim Collection's modern edge, Gallerie dell'Accademia's Renaissance beauties and Punta della Dogana's ambitious installation art. The neighbourhood lazes days away on the sun-drenched Zattere, and convenes in Campo Santa Margherita for spritz (prosecco cocktail) and flirtation. While the eastern tip is heavily tourist focused, it develops a more local feel the further west you go.*

## The Short List

- ***Gallerie dell'Accademia (p64)*** *Getting a crash course in Venetian art at this historic gallery*
- ***Peggy Guggenheim Collection (p66)*** *Schmoozing with Picasso, Pollock and the greats of modern art.*
- ***Basilica di Santa Maria della Salute (p72)*** *Marvelling at mystical architecture and finding hidden Titian masterpieces.*
- ***Ca' Rezzonico (p72)*** *Waltzing through baroque ballrooms, salons and boudoirs festooned in sublime art.*
- ***Punta della Dogana (p72)*** *Comparing fearless contemporary art amid boldly repurposed architecture.*

## Getting There & Around

**Vaporetto** Grand Canal 1, 2 and N lines stop at Accademia; line 1 also calls at Ca' Rezzonico and Salute. Lines 5.1, 5.2, 6 and the N (night) stop at the Zattere and/or San Basilio. Airport lines stop at Zattere.

Dorsoduro & the Accademia Map on p70

Basilica di Santa Maria della Salute (p72) and Grand Canal

Top Experience

# Admire art at Gallerie dell'Accademia

*Hardly academic, these galleries contain more murderous intrigue, forbidden romance and shameless politicking than the most outrageous Venetian parties. The former Scuola della Carità complex maintained its serene composure for centuries, but ever since Napoleon installed his haul of Venetian art trophies here in 1807 – mainly looted from various religious institutions – there's been nonstop visual drama inside these walls.*

MAP P70, E4

041 522 22 47

www.gallerieaccademia.it

Campo de la Carità 1050

adult/reduced €12/2

8.15am-2pm Mon, to 7.15pm Tue-Sun

Accademia

### Carpaccio

UFO arrivals seem imminent in the glowing skies of Carpaccio's gruesome *Crucifixion* and *Glorification of the Ten Thousand Martyrs of Mount Ararat* (Room 2).

### Tintoretto

The Venetian Renaissance master's *Creation of the Animals* (Room 6) is a fantastical bestiary suggesting God put forth his best efforts inventing Venetian seafood (no argument here).

### Titian

His 1576 *Pietà* (Room 6) was possibly finished posthumously by Palma il Giovane, but notice the smears of paint Titian applied with his bare hands and the column-base self-portrait.

### Veronese

Paolo Veronese's restored *Feast in the House of Levi* (Room 10) was originally called *Last Supper*, until Inquisition leaders condemned it for showing dogs and drunkards, among others, cavorting with Apostles. Veronese refused to change a thing besides the title.

### Portrait Galleries

Lock eyes with Lorenzo Lotto's soul-searching *Portrait of a Young Scholar*, Rosalba Carriera's brutally honest self-portrait and Pietro Longhi's lovestruck violinist in *The Dance Lesson*.

### Sala dell'Albergo

The Accademia's grand finale is the Sala dell'Albergo, with a lavishly carved ceiling (pictured), Antonio Vivarini's wraparound 1441–50 masterpiece of fluffy-bearded saints, and Titian's 1534–39 *Presentation of the Virgin*.

### ★ Top Tips

- To skip ahead of the queues in high season, book tickets in advance online (booking fee €1.50).
- Queues are shorter in the afternoon; last entry is 45 minutes before closing, but a proper visit takes at least 1½ hours.
- The audio guide (€6) is mostly descriptive and largely unnecessary – avoid the wait and follow your bliss and the explanatory wall tags.
- Bags larger than 20x30x15cm need to be stored in the lockers, which require a refundable €1 coin.

### Take a Break

Starving artists and gallery-goers descend on Bar alla Toletta (p77) for grilled-to-order *panini*.

## Top Experience

# Visit the palatial Peggy Guggenheim Collection

*After tragically losing her father on the Titanic, heiress Peggy Guggenheim befriended Dadaists, dodged Nazis and changed art history at her palatial home on the Grand Canal. Peggy's Palazzo Venier dei Leoni is a showcase for surrealism, futurism and abstract expressionism by some 200 breakthrough modern artists, including Max Ernst and Jackson Pollock.*

MAP P70, F5

041 240 54 11

www.guggenheim-venice.it

Calle San Cristoforo 701

adult/reduced €15/9

10am-6pm Wed-Mon

Accademia

## Modernist Collection

Peggy Guggenheim escaped Paris two days before the Nazi invasion, and boldly defied established social and artistic dictates. She collected according to her own convictions, featuring folk art and lesser-known artists alongside such radical early modernists as Kandinsky, Picasso, Man Ray, Rothko, Mondrian, Joseph Cornell and Dalí.

## Italian Avant-Garde

Upon her 1948 arrival in Venice, Peggy became a spirited advocate for contemporary Italian art, which had largely gone out of favour with the rise of Mussolini and the partisan politics of WWII. Her support led to reappraisals of Umberto Boccioni, Giorgio Morandi, Giacomo Balla, Giuseppe Capogrossi and Giorgio de Chirico, and aided Venice's own Emilio Vedova and Giuseppe Santomaso. Never afraid to make a splash, Peggy gave passing gondoliers an eyeful on her Grand Canal quay: Marino Marini's 1948 *Angel of the City,* a bronze male nude on horseback visibly excited by the possibilities on the horizon.

## Sculpture Garden

Peggy's palace was never finished, but that didn't stop her from filling every space indoors and out with art. In the sculpture garden, wander past bronzes by Henry Moore, Alberto Giacometti and Constantin Brancusci, Yoko Ono's *Wish Tree* and a shiny black-granite lump by Anish Kapoor. The city of Venice granted an honorary dispensation for Peggy to be buried beneath the Giacometti sculptures, alongside her dearly departed lapdogs.

## ★ Top Tips

- Excellent audio guides (€7) are available in Italian, English, German, French and Spanish.
- Free daily presentations in Italian and English are given on the life of Peggy Guggenheim (noon and 4pm) and individual works in the collection (11am and 5pm).
- You're required to store your bags in the free lockers near the ticket office.
- If you spot someone wearing an 'Ask me about the Art' badge, feel free to quiz them. They're Guggenheim interns in training.
- Free Kids' Day workshops (mainly in Italian) are held on Sundays at 3pm for children aged from four to 10.

## Take a Break

The gallery's pavilion **cafe** offers respectable espresso, light lunches and high tea with views over the sculpture garden.

Walking Tour

# Happy Hour in Campo Santa Margherita

*By day Campo Santa Margherita hosts a weekday fish market, the odd flea market and periodic political protests, but by six o'clock this unruly square becomes Venice's nightlife hub. Just don't try to pack it all into one happy hour. Pace yourself on your giro d'ombra (pub crawl), lest you end up in the drink of a nearby canal.*

**Start** Bakarò do Draghi; vaporetto Ca' Rezzonico

**Finish** Orient Experience II; vaporetto Ca' Rezzonico

**Length** 700m; 25 minutes

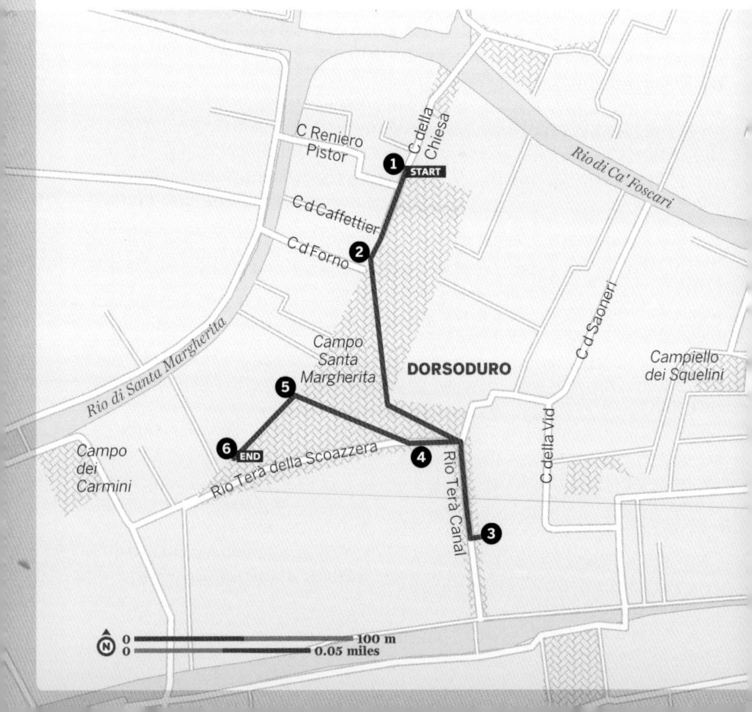

### ❶ Snacks at Bakarò

*'Permesso!'* (Pardon!) is the chorus inside this historic **bar** (041 241 27 58; www.bakaro.it; Campo Santa Margherita 3665; 10am-1am; Ca' Rezzonico), where the crowd spills onto the sidewalk and tries not to spill drinks in the process. Arrive at the tiny wooden bar early for the best choice of 45-plus wines.

### ❷ Spritz at Il Caffè Rosso

Locals affectionately call this red **storefront** (041 528 79 98; www.cafferosso.it; Campo Santa Margherita 2963; 7am-1am Mon-Sat; ; Ca' Rezzonico) *'al rosso'* (the red), and its inexpensive *spritz* (*prosecco* cocktail) generously splashed with scarlet Aperol gives visitors and locals alike an instant flush of Venetian colour.

### ❸ Cocktails at Imagina Café

For your next stop, branch out to top-shelf cocktails served at this sleek, backlit **bar** (041 241 06 25; www.imaginacafe.it; Rio Terà Canal 3126; 7am-9pm Sun-Thu, to 1am Fri & Sat; ; Ca' Rezzonico) surrounded by local art. The creative, chatty and gay-friendly crowd here should probably start paying rent at outdoor tables, while their sweater-clad dogs bask in the admiration of passers-by.

### ❹ Ice Cream Fit for a Doge at Gelateria Il Doge

If you're wondering hat the crowd is at the southern end of the *campo*, it's the mob eyeing up the impossibly good selection of gelato at this venerable **ice-cream parlour** (389 1288965; www.gelateriaildoge.com; Campo Santa Margherita 3058a; scoops from €1.80; 8am-11pm; ; Ca' Rezzonico). Have a bar break and join the gang shouting out orders for pink Himalayan salt, fig and caramel swirl and refreshing Sicilian lemon *granita* (sorbet).

### ❺ Flirting at Osteria alla Bifora

While *spritz*-pounding students carouse outside in the *campo*, gentle flirting ensues in this chandelier-lit medieval **wine cave** (041 523 61 19; Campo Santa Margherita 2930; noon-2am; Ca' Rezzonico) over big-hearted Veneto merlot. While you wait for a platter of cheese and carved-to-order cured meats to arrive, you'll make newfound friends at communal tables.

### ❻ Late-Night Munchies at Orient Experience II

This wildly popular **Eastern deli** (041 520 02 17; www.facebook.com/orientexperiencevenezia; Campo Santa Margherita 2928; meals €12-18; 10am-11.30pm; Ca' Rezzonico), run by Ahmed, dishes up colourful bowls of Afghan, Iranian, Turkish and Maghrebi cuisine to hungry students, curious Venetians and adventurous travellers. Round it all off with a delicious cup of cardamom coffee and some pistachio baklava.

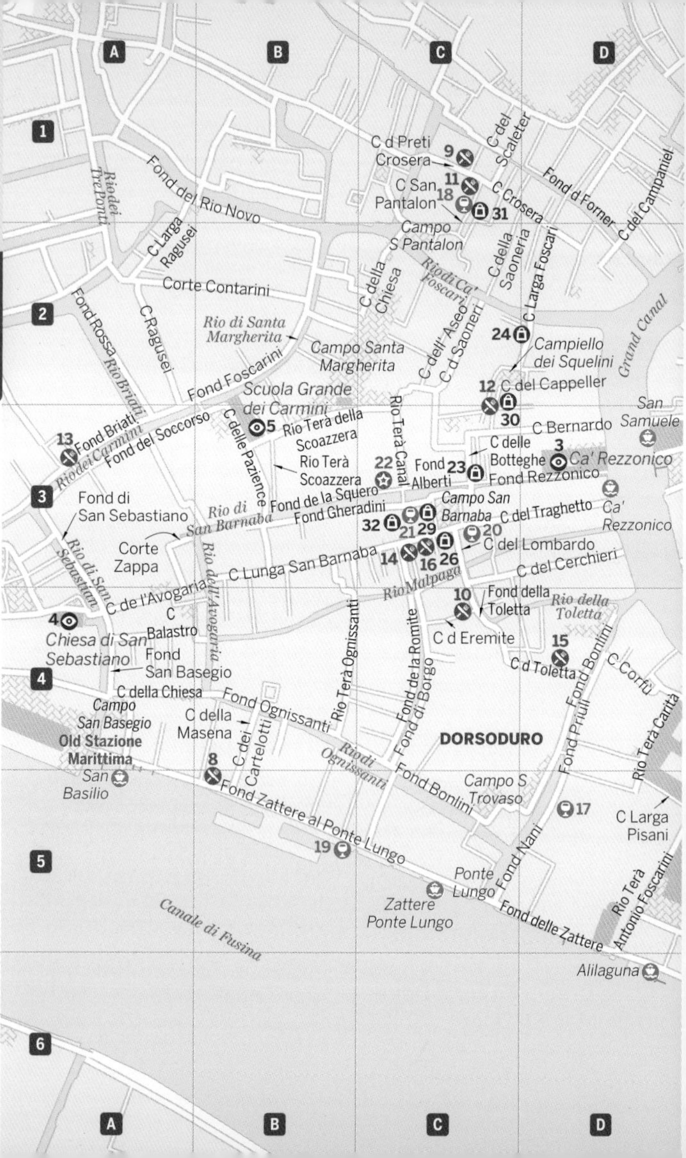
A
B
C
D
1
2
3
4
5
6
C d Preti Crosera
9
11
C San Pantalon
18
31
C del Scaleter
C Crosera
Fond d Forner
C del Campaniel
Campo S Pantalon
Rio dei Tre Ponti
Fond del Rio Novo
C Larga Ragusei
Corte Contarini
Fond Rossa
Rio Briati
C Ragusei
Rio di Santa Margherita
Campo Santa Margherita
C della Chiesa
Rio di Ca' Foscari
C della Saoneria
C Larga Foscari
C dell' Aseo
C d Saoneri
24
Campiello dei Squelini
Grand Canal
12
C del Cappeller
30
San Samuele
Fond Foscarini
Scuola Grande dei Carmini
5
Rio Terà della Scoazzera
Rio Terà Scoazzera
C delle Pazienze
Rio Terà Canal
13
Fond Briati
Rio dei Carmini
Fond del Soccorso
C Bernardo
C delle Botteghe
3
Ca' Rezzonico
22
Fond Alberti
23
Fond Rezzonico
Fond di San Sebastiano
Rio di San Barnaba
Fond de la Squero
Fond Gheradini
Campo San Barnaba
C del Traghetto
Ca' Rezzonico
32
21
29
20
Corte Zappa
Rio di San Sebastian
C Lunga San Barnaba
14
16
26
C del Lombardo
C del Cerchieri
Rio Malpaga
C de l'Avogaria
Rio dell'Avogaria
10
Fond della Toletta
Rio della Toletta
4
Chiesa di San Sebastiano
C Balastro
Fond San Basegio
C d Eremite
15
C d Toletta
Fond Bonlini
C Corfù
C della Chiesa
Campo San Basegio
Old Stazione Marittima
San Basilio
C della Masena
C dei Cartelotti
Fond Ognissanti
Rio Terà Ognissanti
Fond de la Romite
Fond di Borgo
DORSODURO
Fond Priuli
Rio Terà Carità
8
Rio di Ognissanti
Fond Bonlini
Campo S Trovaso
17
C Larga Pisani
Fond Zattere al Ponte Lungo
19
Fond Nani
Ponte Lungo
Zattere Ponte Lungo
Canale di Fusina
Fond delle Zattere
Rio Terà Antonio Foscarini
Alilaguna

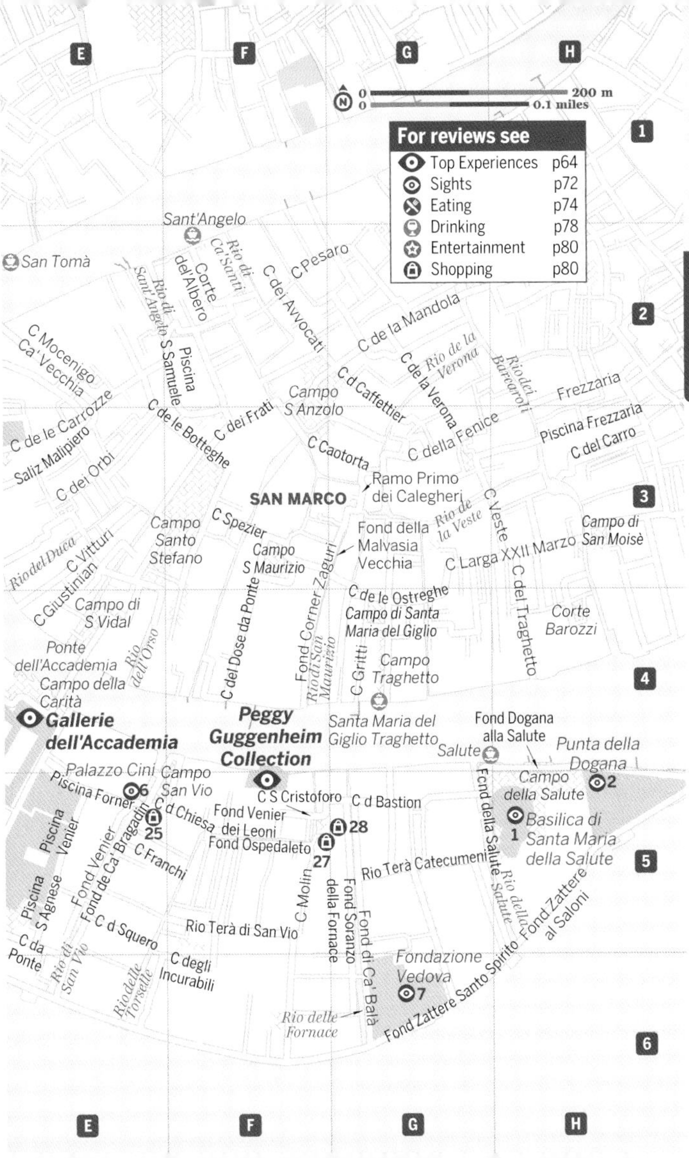
E
F
G
H
1
2
3
4
5
6
0 200 m
0 0.1 miles
For reviews see
Top Experiences p64
Sights p72
Eating p74
Drinking p78
Entertainment p80
Shopping p80
Sant'Angelo
San Tomà
Rio di Ca' Santi
Corte dell'Albero
Rio di Sant'Angelo
C Pesaro
C dei Avvocati
C de la Mandola
C Mocenigo Ca' Vecchia
Piscina S Samuele
Rio de la Verona
Rio dei Barcaroli
C de la Verona
C d Caffettier
Campo S Anzolo
Frezzaria
C de le Carrozze
C de le Botteghe
C dei Frati
C della Fenice
Piscina Frezzaria
C del Carro
Saliz Malipiero
C Caotorta
C dei Orbi
Ramo Primo dei Calegheri
SAN MARCO
C Veste
Rio de la Veste
Campo di San Moisè
Campo Santo Stefano
C Spezier
Fond della Malvasia Vecchia
Rio del Duca
C Vitturi
Campo S Maurizio
C Larga XXII Marzo
C Giustinian
C de le Ostreghe
Campo di S Vidal
C del Dose da Ponte
Fond Corner Zaguri
Campo di Santa Maria del Giglio
C del Traghetto
Corte Barozzi
Ponte dell'Accademia
Rio dell'Orso
Rio di San Maurizio
C Gritti
Campo Traghetto
Campo della Carità
Gallerie dell'Accademia
Peggy Guggenheim Collection
Santa Maria del Giglio Traghetto
Fond Dogana alla Salute
Salute
Punta della Dogana
Palazzo Cini
Campo San Vio
6
Campo della Salute
2
Piscina Forner
C S Cristoforo
C d Bastion
C d Chiesa
Fond Venier dei Leoni
28
Basilica di Santa Maria della Salute
1
Fond della Salute
25
Fond Ospedaleto
27
Piscina Venier
C Franchi
Fond Venier
Fond de Ca' Bragadin
Rio Terà Catecumeni
Rio della Salute
Fond Zattere al Saloni
Piscina S Agnese
C Molin
della Fornace
Fond Soranzo
C d Squero
Rio Terà di San Vio
Fond di Ca' Balà
C da Ponte
Rio di San Vio
C degli Incurabili
Fondazione Vedova
7
Fond Zattere Santo Spirito
Rio delle Torselle
Rio delle Fornace
E
F
G
H

## Sights

### Basilica di Santa Maria della Salute BASILICA

1 MAP P70, H5

Baldassare Longhena's magnificent basilica is prominently positioned near the entrance to the Grand Canal, its white stones, exuberant statuary and high domes gleaming spectacularly under the sun. The church makes good on an official appeal by the Venetian Senate directly to the Madonna in 1630, after 80,000 Venetians had been killed by plague. The Senate promised the Madonna a church in exchange for her intervention on behalf of Venice – no expense or effort spared. (Our Lady of Health Basilica; www.basilicasalutevenezia.it; Campo de la Salute 1; sacristy adult/reduced €4/2; 9.30am-noon & 3-5.30pm; Salute)

### Punta della Dogana GALLERY

2 MAP P70, H5

Fortuna, the weathervane atop Punta della Dogana, swung Venice's way in 2005, when bureaucratic hassles in Paris convinced art collector François Pinault to showcase his works in Venice's long-abandoned customs warehouses. Built by Giuseppe Benoni in 1677 to ensure no ship entered the Grand Canal without paying duties, the warehouses reopened in 2009 after a striking reinvention by Japanese architect Tadao Ando. The space now hosts exhibitions of ambitious, large-scale artworks from some of the world's most provocative creative minds. (041 200 10 57; www.palazzograssi.it; Fondamenta Salute 2; adult/reduced €15/10, incl Palazzo Grassi €18/15; 10am-7pm Wed-Mon Apr-Nov; Salute)

### Ca' Rezzonico MUSEUM

3 MAP P70, D3

Baroque dreams come true at this Baldassare Longhena–designed Grand Canal *palazzo* (mansion), where a marble staircase leads to a vast gilded **ballroom** and sumptuous salons filled with period furniture, paintings, porcelain and mesmerising ceiling frescoes, four of which were painted by Giambattista Tiepolo. The building was largely stripped of its finery when the Rezzonico family departed in 1810, but this was put right after the city acquired it in 1935, and refurnished it with pieces salvaged from other decaying palaces. (Museum of 18th-Century Venice; 041 241 01 00; www.visitmuve.it; Fondamenta Rezzonico 3136; adult/reduced €10/7.50, or with Museum Pass; 10am-5pm Wed-Mon; Ca' Rezzonico)

### Chiesa di San Sebastiano CHURCH

4 MAP P70, A4

Antonio Scarpignano's relatively austere 1508–48 facade creates a sense of false modesty at this neighbourhood church. The interior is adorned with floor-to-ceiling masterpieces by Paolo Veronese, executed over three decades. According to popular local legend, Veronese found sanctuary at San Sebastiano in 1555 after fleeing murder charges in Verona, and his works in this church deliver lavish thanks to the parish and an especially brilliant poke in the eye to his accusers. (St Sebastian's Church; www.chorusvenezia.org; Campo San Sebastian 1687; adult/reduced €3/1.50, free with Chorus Pass; 10.30am-4.30pm Mon-Sat; San Basilio)

### Scuola Grande dei Carmini HISTORIC BUILDING

5 MAP P70, B3

Seventeenth-century backpackers must have thought they'd died and gone to heaven at this magnificent confraternity clubhouse, dedicated to Our Lady of Mt Carmel, with its lavish interiors by Giambattista Tiepolo and Baldassare Longhena. The gold-leafed, Longhena-designed stucco stairway heads up towards Tiepolo's nine-panel ceiling of a rosy *Virgin in Glory*. The adjoining hostel room is bedecked in marble and *boiserie* (wood carving). (041 528 94 20; www.scuolagrandecarmini.it; Campo Santa Margherita 2617; adult/reduced €7/5; 11am-5pm; Ca' Rezzonico)

### Palazzo Cini GALLERY

6 MAP P70, E5

This elegant 16th-century Gothic *palazzo* was the former home of industrialist and philanthropist Vittorio Cini, who filled it with

Ceiling fresco, Ca'Rezzonico

first-class paintings, period furnishings, ceramics and Murano glass. Wonderful paintings by lesser-known Renaissance lights such as Filippo Lippi, Piero di Cosimo and Dosso Dossi cover the walls, their glowing brilliance having even more impact in these intimate, domestic spaces. (☎041 241 12 81; www.palazzocini.it; Piscina Forner 864; adult/reduced €10/8; ⏰11am-7pm Wed-Mon May-Nov; ⛴Accademia)

### Fondazione Vedova GALLERY

7 MAP P70, G6

A retrofit designed by Pritzker Prize–winning architect Renzo Piano transformed Venice's historic salt warehouses into art galleries. Although the facade is from the 1830s, the warehouses were established in the 14th century, when the all-important salt monopoly secured Venice's fortune. The repurposing of the buildings is only fitting, now that the city's most precious commodity is art. They're only open for exhibitions staged by the foundation formed in honour of Venetian painter Emilio Vedova; check the website for details. (Magazzini del Sale; ☎041 522 66 26; www.fondazionevedova.org; Fondamenta Zattere ai Saloni 266; adult/reduced €8/4; ⏰10.30am-6pm Wed-Sun during exhibitions; ⛴Spirito Santo)

## Eating

### Riviera ITALIAN €€€

8 MAP P70, B5

A former rock musician, GP Cremonini now focuses his

Fondazione Vedova

JO-ANN TITMARSH/LONELY PLANET ©

## Grand Canal Bling & Bogeymen

As magnificent as the Grand Canal remains, it was once even more colourful – with Giorgione and Titian frescoes gracing the facade of the **Fondaco dei Tedeschi** (www.dfs.com; Calle del Fontego dei Tedeschi 5350; ⏲10am-8pm; ⛴Rialto), and gold leaf glistening from the **Ca' d'Oro** (p122). Yet that didn't stop aristocratic noses being put out of joint when a pair of Murano glass companies decided to pimp their Grand Canal headquarters with golden mosaics in the late 19th and early 20th centuries. **Palazzo Barbarigo** dates to the 16th century but gained its glitzy wrapping in 1886, featuring images of glass blowers displaying their work to architects and the doge himself. **Palazzo Salviati** followed suit in 1924, with a large central mosaic of a blonde effigy of Venice enthroned in splendour. You can easily spot them as you cruise along the canal between the Guggenheim and La Salute.

Close by is **Ca' Dario** (Ramo Ca' Dario 352; ⛴Salute), a 15th-century palazzo with three levels of arched windows abutted by three oculi surrounded by disks of coloured marble. Its mesmerising reflection was once painted by Claude Monet, but it's famous for a more nefarious reason: starting with the daughter of its original owner, Giovanni Dario, an unusual number of its occupants have met untimely deaths. Gossips claim this effectively dissuaded Woody Allen from buying the house in the late 1990s. The former manager of The Who, Kit Lambert, moved out after complaining of being hounded by the palace's ghosts, and was found dead shortly after in 1981. One week after renting the place for a holiday in 2002, The Who's bass player, John Entwhistle, died of a heart attack. Look for it just past the first small canal to the left of the Guggenheim.

considerable talents on ensuring his top-end restaurant – Dorsoduro's finest – delivers exemplary service and perfectly cooked seafood: think homemade pasta with scallops or sea-bass poached with prawns. The setting, overlooking the Giudecca Canal, is similarly spectacular. For serious gourmands, the 11-course tasting menu (€150) with wine pairings (€55) is an unmissable experience. (☎041 522 76 21; www.ristoranteriviera.it; Fondamenta Zattere al Ponte Lungo 1473; meals €67-157; ⏲12.30-3pm & 7-10.30pm Fri-Tue; ⛴Zattere)

### Estro INTERNATIONAL **€€**

9 MAP P70, C1

Estro is anything you want it to be: wine bar, *aperitivo* pit stop or sit-down degustation restaurant. The

## Sacred Music at Salute

If you think the Longhena-designed dome of the **Basilica di Santa Maria della Salute** (p72) looks magnificent, wait until you hear how it sounds. Weekdays at 3.30pm, vespers are played on the basilica's organ, dating from 1783. These musical interludes are free, and the acoustics are nothing short of celestial.

vast selection of wine was chosen by young-gun owners Alberto and Dario, whose passion for quality extends to the food – from *baccalà mantecato* (creamed cod) on polenta crisps, to guinea-fowl lasagne or a succulent burger dripping with Asiago cheese. (041 476 49 14; www.estrovenezia.com; Calle Crosera 3778; meals €32-47; noon-11pm Wed-Mon; ; San Tomà)

### Enoteca ai Artisti ITALIAN €€€

10 MAP P70, C4

Dishes might include a lightly curried rabbit *maltagliati* (cut pasta) or beef cheeks with polenta chips at this elegant *enoteca* (wine-orientated bistro), paired with exceptional wines by the glass. Sidewalk tables make for great people-watching, but book ahead as space is limited inside and out. Note: only turf (no surf) dishes on Mondays, as the fish market is closed. (041 523 89 44; www.enotecaartisti.com; Fondamenta de la Toletta 1169a; meals €48-55; 12.45-2.30pm & 7-10pm Mon-Sat; Ca' Rezzonico)

### Pasticceria Tonolo PASTRIES €

11 MAP P70, C1

Long, skinny Tonolo is the stuff of local legend, a fact confirmed by the never-ending queue of customers. Ditch packaged B&B croissants for flaky apple strudel, velvety *bignè al zabaione* (marsala cream pastry) and oozing chocolate croissants. Devour one at the bar with a bracing espresso, then bag another for the road. (041 523 72 09; http://pasticceria-tonolo-venezia.business.site; Calle San Pantalon 3764; pastries €1-4; 7.30am-8pm Tue-Sat, to 1pm Sun; Ca' Rezzonico)

### Do Farai VENETIAN €€

12 MAP P70, C3

Venetian regulars pack this crimson wood-panelled room, decorated with Regata Storica victory pendants and Murano glass decanters. The mixed antipasto is a succulent prologue to classic Venetian dishes like pasta with shellfish, grilled *orata* (bream), *fegato alla veneziana* (veal liver with onions on polenta) and *sarde in saor* (sardines in a tangy onion marinade). (041 277 03 69; Calle del Capeler 3278; meals €32-47; noon-2.30pm & 7-10.30pm Mon-Sat; Ca' Rezzonico)

## Da Codroma VENETIAN €€

13 MAP P70, A3

In a city plagued by high prices and indifferent eating experiences, the shared wooden tables at Da Codroma are the perfect dining antidote. Chef Nicola faithfully maintains Venetian traditions here, serving up *il saor* (cured sardines and prawns), *bigoli in salsa* (buckwheat pasta with anchovy and onions) and delicious semifreddo to locals and savvy tourists alike. (041 524 67 89; www.facebook.com/dacodroma; Fondamenta Briati 2540; meals €34-42; 10am-4pm & 6-11pm Tue-Sat; ; San Basilio)

## La Bitta VENETIAN €€

14 MAP P70, C3

Venice is known for its seafood but this cosy, woody bistro taps into the other side of the cuisine, serving a concise menu focused on meat and seasonal veggies. It's one of the best places in town to try the classic *fegato alla veneziana* (veal liver with onions). Reservations recommended; cash only. (041 523 05 31; Calle Lunga San Barnaba 2753a; meals €34-37; 7-10.30pm Mon-Sat; ; Ca' Rezzonico)

## Toletta Snack-Bar SANDWICHES €

15 MAP P70, D4

Midway through museum crawls from Accademia to Ca' Rezzonico, Toletta satisfies starving artists

Pasticceria Tonolo

Demijohns of Venetian wine

with lip-smacking, grilled-to-order *panini* (sandwiches), including *prosciutto crudo* (dry-cured ham), rocket and mozzarella, and daily vegetarian options. *Tramezzini* (triangular stacked sandwiches) are tasty too. Get yours to go, or grab a seat for around €1 more. (041 520 01 96; Sacca de la Toletta 1191; sandwiches €1.60-5; 7am-8pm; ; Ca' Rezzonico)

### Osteria ai 4 Feri VENETIAN €€

16 MAP P70, C3

Adorned with artworks by some well-known creative fans, this honest, good-humoured *osteria* (casual tavern) is well known for its simple, classic seafood dishes like *spaghetti con seppie* (with cuttlefish), grilled *orata* (sea bream) and tender calamari. Post-meal coffees are made using a traditional Italian percolator for that homely, old-school feeling. No credit cards. (041 520 69 78; Calle Lunga San Barnaba 2754a; meals €27-34; 12.30-2.30pm & 7-10.30pm Mon-Sat; Ca' Rezzonico)

## Drinking

### Cantine del Vino già Schiavi VENETIAN €

17 MAP P70, D5

It may look like a wine shop and function as a bar, but this legendary canalside spot also serves the best *cicheti* (Venetian tapas) on this side of the Grand Canal. Choose from the impressive counter selection or ask for a filled-to-order roll. Chaos cheerfully prevails, with an eclectic cast of locals propping up the bar. (041 523 00 34; www.cantinaschiavi.com; Fondamenta Priuli 992; cicheti €1.50; 8.30am-8.30pm Mon-Sat; Zattere)

## El Sbarlefo BAR

18 MAP P70, C1

If you're looking to escape the raucous student scene on Campo Santa Margherita, head to this chic bar with its sophisticated soundtrack, high-quality *cicheti* (Venetian tapas) and live music on the weekends. Aside from the long list of regional wines, there's a serious selection of spirits here. (041 524 66 50; www.elsbarlefo.it; Calle San Pantalon 3757; 10am-11pm; ; San Tomà)

## El Chioschetto BAR

19 MAP P70, B5

There's really no better place to park yourself for *aperitivo* than at this pint-sized kiosk on the Zattere overlooking the Giudecca Canal. Even on frosty spring evenings the tables fill up with a mixed crowd downing cocktails and *spritzes* and watching the spectacular Venetian sunset. In summer, on Wednesday and Saturday evenings, there's even live music. (348 3968466; Fondamenta Zattere al Ponte Lungo 1406a; 8.30am-2am Mar-Oct, 9am-5pm Nov-Feb; Zattere)

## Ai Artisti BAR

20 MAP P70, C3

True to its name, artsy student types pack out this cafe-bar on the weekends and spill out onto the street outside. It's been serving drinks and snacks since 1897, and retains a local feel despite the city's shifting demographics. (393 9680135; Campo San Barnaba 2771; 8am-midnight; Ca' Rezzonico)

## Osteria ai Pugni BAR

21 MAP P70, C3

Centuries ago, brawls on the bridge out the front inevitably ended in the canal, but now Venetians settle differences with one of over 50 wines by the glass at this ever-packed bar, pimped with recycled Magnum-bottle lamps

*Cicheti* and wine

### Traghetto Crossing

Hop across the Grand Canal with the locals on the San Marco *traghetto* (passenger gondola), which connects Santa Maria del Giglio, 500m west of Piazza San Marco, to the Basilica di Santa Maria della Salute (San Gregorio stop), saving you a 40-minute walk. It costs €2 each way.

and wine-crate tables. The latest drops are listed on the blackboard, with *aperitivo*-friendly nibbles including *polpette* (meatballs) and cured local meats on bread. (☎346 9607785; www.osteriaaipugni.com; Fondamenta Gherardini 2856; ⏲8am-11pm Mon-Sat, 10am-11pm Sun; ⛴Ca' Rezzonico)

# Entertainment

### Venice Jazz Club JAZZ

22 MAP P70, C3

Jazz is alive and swinging in Dorsoduro, where the resident VJC Jazz Quartet takes to the stage on Mondays, Wednesday and Saturdays, while the VJC Latin Jazz & Bossa Nova Quartet takes over on Tuesdays and Thursdays; shows start at 9pm. The venue closes for August, December and January, and much of February. (☎041 523 20 56; www.venicejazzclub.com; Fondamenta del Squero 3102; admission incl 1st drink €20; ⏲7-11pm Mon-Wed, Fri & Sat; 📶; ⛴Ca' Rezzonico)

# Shopping

### Ca' Macana ARTS & CRAFTS

23 MAP P70, C3

Glimpse the talents behind the Venetian Carnevale masks that impressed Stanley Kubrick so much he ordered several for his final film *Eyes Wide Shut*. Choose your papier-mâché persona from the selection of coquettish courtesan's eye-shades, chequered Casanova disguises and long-nosed plague doctor masks – or decorate your own at Ca' Macana's mask-painting workshops (from €39). (☎041 520 32 29; www.camacana.com; Calle de le Botteghe 3172; ⏲10am-8pm summer, to 6.30pm winter; ⛴Ca' Rezzonico)

### Paolo Olbi ARTS & CRAFTS

24 MAP P70, C2

Thoughts worth committing to paper deserve Paolo Olbi's keepsake books, albums and stationery, whose fans include Hollywood actors and NYC mayors (ask to see the guestbook). Ordinary journals can't compare to Olbi originals, handmade with heavyweight paper and bound with exquisite leather bindings. The watercolour postcards of Venice make for beautiful, bargain souvenirs. (☎041 523 76 55; www.olbi.atspace.com; Calle Foscari 3253; ⏲10.30am-12.40pm & 3.30-7.30pm Mar-Dec, 3.30-7.30pm Jan & Feb; ⛴San Tomà)

### Marina e Susanna Sent

GLASS

25 MAP P70, E5

Wearable waterfalls and soap-bubble necklaces are Venice-style signatures, thanks to the Murano-born Sent sisters. Defying centuries-old beliefs that women can't handle molten glass, their minimalist art-glass statement jewellery is featured in museum stores worldwide, from Palazzo Grassi to MoMA. See new collections at this store, their flagship Murano studio (p157), or the San Marco and San Polo branches. (041 520 81 36; www.marinaesusannasent.com; Campo San Vio 669; 10am-6.30pm; Accademia)

### Madera

DESIGN

26 MAP P70, C3

Restyle your life at this modern design showcase, which stocks a sharply curated selection of Italian and international jewellery, accessories, homewares and gifts. The emphasis is on handmade and harder-to-find objects, whether it's sculptural chopping blocks and necklaces, or geometric serving trays and bags. (393 9936938; www.maderavenezia.it; Campo San Barnaba 2762; 10am-1pm & 3.30-7.30pm Tue-Sat; Ca' Rezzonico)

### Claudia Canestrelli

ANTIQUES

27 MAP P70, F5

Hand-coloured lithographs of fanciful lagoon fish, 19th-century miniatures of cats dressed as

Musicians in Piazza San Marco (p47)

LI SEN/SHUTTERSTOCK ©

Murano glass

generals, and vintage cufflinks make for charming souvenirs of Venice's past in this walk-in curio cabinet. Collector-artisan Claudia Canestrelli brings back bygone elegance with her repurposed antique earrings, including free-form baroque pearls dangling from gilded bronze elephants. (340 5776089; Campiello Barbaro 364a; 11am-1pm & 3-5pm Mon-Sat; Salute)

### Le Fórcole di Saverio Pastor

ARTS & CRAFTS

28 MAP P70, G5

Only one thing actually moves like Jagger: Mick Jagger's bespoke *fórcola,* hand-carved by Saverio Pastor. Each forked wooden gondola oarlock is individually designed to match a gondolier's height, weight and movement, so the gondola doesn't rock too hard when the gondolier hits a groove. Pastor's miniature *fórcole* twist elegantly, striking an easy balance on gondolas and mantelpieces alike. (041 522 56 99; www.forcole.com; Fondamenta Soranzo detta de la Fornace 341; 8.30am-6pm Mon-Fri; Salute)

### Signor Blum

TOYS

29 MAP P70, C3

Kids may have to drag adults away from the 2D wooden puzzles of the Rialto Bridge and grinning wooden duckies before these clever handmade toys induce acute cases of nostalgia. Mobiles made of colourful carved gondola prows would seem equally at home in an arty foyer and a nursery. And did we mention the Venice-themed clocks? (041 522 63 67; www.signorblum.com; Campo San Barnaba 2840; 10am-1.30pm & 2.30-7.30pm Mon-Sat; Ca' Rezzonico)

## Danghyra

CERAMICS

30 MAP P70, C2

Spare white bisque cups seem perfect for a Zen tea ceremony, but look inside – that iridescent lilac glaze is pure Carnevale. Danghyra's striking ceramics are hand-thrown in Venice with a magic touch: her platinum-glazed bowls make the simplest pasta dish fit for a modern-day doge. (041 522 41 95; www.danghyra.com; Calle del Capeler 3220; 10am-1pm & 3-7pm Tue-Sun; Ca' Rezzonico)

## Acqua Marea

SHOES

31 MAP P70, C1

Question: how do you maintain a *bella figura* (good impression) when high tides are sloshing around your ankles? The answer can be found at Martina Ranaldo's delightful store, where you can find rubber boots in lemon yellow and floral prints, ingenious two-tone rubber spats, ankle boots with coloured soles and comfortable non-leather walking shoes. (351 9221895; www.facebook.com/acquamarea; Calle San Pantalon 3750; noon-7pm Mon-Fri; San Tomà)

## Papuni Art

JEWELLERY

32 MAP P70, C3

Venice artisan Ninfa Salerno gives staid pearl strands a sense of humour with bouncy black rubber, weaves fuchsia rubber discs into glowing UFO necklaces, and embeds Murano glass beads in rubber daisy cocktail rings. (041 241 04 34; www.papuniart.it; Fondamenta Gheradini 2834a; 11am-7pm Mon & Thu-Sat, 3-7pm Tue & Wed; Ca' Rezzonico)

VE 9503

# Explore San Polo & Santa Croce

*Heavenly devotion and earthly delights co-exist in these twinned neighbourhoods, where divine art rubs up against the ancient red-light district, now home to artisan workshops and wine bars. Don't miss Titian's glowing Madonna at I Frari and Tintorettos at Scuola Grande di San Rocco. Grand Canal museums showcase fashion and natural history, while island produce fills the Rialto Market.*

## The Short List

- ***Scuola Grande di San Rocco (p86)*** *Seeing lightning strike at this opulent confraternity clubhouse covered with dramatic Tintoretto paintings.*
- ***I Frari (p88)*** *Watching Titian's red-hot Madonna light up this soaring Gothic basilica.*
- ***Rialto Market (p90)*** *Working up an appetite over lagoon surf and turf at this produce-bursting market.*
- ***Ca' Pesaro (p98)*** *Ping-ponging between modern masterpieces and Japanese antiques in an ostentatious Grand Canal palace.*
- ***Scuola Grande di San Giovanni Evangelista (p98)*** *Taking over-the-top interior-design cues from some of Venice's top architects and artists.*

## Getting There & Around

**Vaporetto** Most call at Piazzale Roma in Santa Croce. For Santa Croce sights, San Stae, served by lines 1 and N, is most convenient. Lines 1 and N also service Rialto-Mercato and San Tomà in San Polo.

San Polo & Santa Croce Map on p96

**Gondola outside Rialto Market (p90)** GOZZOLI/SHUTTERSTOCK ©

Top Experience

# Tour Tintoretto at Scuola Grande di San Rocco

*You'll swear the paint is still fresh on the 50 action-packed Tintorettos completed between 1575 and 1587 for this confraternity meeting house, dedicated to St Roch, the patron of the plague-stricken. Tintoretto painted nail-biting scenes of looming despair and last-minute redemption, illuminating a survivor's struggle with breathtaking urgency.*

MAP P96, B5

041 523 48 64

www.scuolagrandesanrocco.org

Campo San Rocco 3052

adult/reduced €10/8

9.30am-5.30pm

San Tomà

### Assembly Hall

Downstairs in the assembly hall are works by Venetian A-list artists including Titian, Giorgione and Tiepolo. But Tintoretto steals the show with the story of the Virgin Mary, starting on the left wall with *Annunciation*, where the angel surprises Mary at her sewing. The cycle ends with a dark, cataclysmic *Ascension* (pictured), unlike Titian's glowing version at I Frari.

### Sala Grande Superiore

Take the grand **Scarpagnino staircase** to the Sala Grande Superiore, where you may be seized with a powerful instinct to duck, given all the action in the **Old Testament ceiling scenes** – you can almost hear the swoop overhead as a winged angel dives to nourish the ailing prophet in *Elijah Fed by an Angel*. Meanwhile, eerie illumination ominously strikes subjects in dark **New Testament wall scenes**. When Tintoretto painted these scenes, the plague had just taken 50,000 Venetians, and the cause of and cure were unknown. With dynamic lines pointing to glimmers of hope on still-distant horizons, Tintoretto created a moving parable for epidemics through the ages.

### Sala Albergo

The New Testament cycle ends with the *Crucifixion* in the Sala Albergo, where things suddenly begin to look up – literally. Every Venetian artist who'd survived the plague wanted the commission to paint this building, so Tintoretto cheated a little. Instead of producing sketches like his rival Paolo Veronese, he painted this magnificent *tondo* (ceiling panel) and dedicated it to the saint, knowing that such a gift couldn't be refused, or matched by other artists.

### ★ Top Tips

- From spring to late autumn, the artworks provide a bewitching backdrop to top-notch classical-music concerts. Check the website for details.
- Grab a mirror to avoid neck strain when you view Tintoretto's ceiling panels in the upstairs halls.
- The feast of St Roch (16 August) is celebrated with a solemn Mass and procession around the Campo San Rocco.

### Take a Break

Celebrate Venice's survival against the odds with a coffee or *prosecco* at Basegò (p106).

Break for superior gourmet *panini* away from the crowds at Snack Bar Ai Nomboli (p104).

Top Experience

# Go Gothic at I Frari

*As you've no doubt heard, there's a Titian – make that the Titian – altarpiece at the Friary. But the 14th-century Gothic basilica is itself a towering achievement, with a heaven-scraping ceiling, intricate marquetry choir stalls and a succession of grandiose monuments lining its high brick walls. While Canova's white-marble tomb appears permanently moonlit, Titian's Assunta seems to shed its own sunlight.*

MAP P96, C5

Basilica di Santa Maria Gloriosa dei Frari

041 272 86 18

www.basilicadeifrari.it

Campo dei Frari 3072, San Polo

adult/reduced €3/1.50, with Chorus Pass free

9am-6pm Mon-Sat, 1-6pm Sun

San Tomà

## Assunta

Visitors are inexorably drawn to the front of this cavernous Gothic church by a 6.7m by 3.4m altarpiece that seems to glow from within. This is Titian's 1518 *Assunta* (Assumption), capturing the split second the radiant Madonna reaches heavenward, finds her footing on a cloud, and escapes this mortal coil in a dramatic swirl of red and blue robes. Both inside and outside the painting, onlookers gasp and point at the glorious, glowing sight. Titian outdid himself here, upstaging even his own 1526 Pesaro altarpiece – a dreamlike composite family portrait of the Madonna and Child with the Venetian Pesaro family. You'll find it on the fourth altar on the left nave.

## Other Masterpieces

As though this weren't quite enough artistic achievement, there's puzzlework marquetry worthy of MC Escher in the **coro** (choir stalls), Bellini's achingly sweet *Madonna with Child* triptych in the **sacristy**, and Bartolomeo Vivarini's *St Mark Enthroned* in the **Capella Corner**.

In the middle of the nave, Baldassare Longhena's **Doge Pesaro funereal monument** is hoisted by four black-marble figures bursting from ragged clothes like Invincible Hulks. Bringing up the rear are disconsolate mourners dabbing at their eyes on Canova's **pyramid mausoleum** (pictured), originally intended as a monument to Titian. The great painter was lost to the plague at the age of 90 in 1576, but legend has it that, in light of his contributions here, Venice's strict rules of quarantine were bent to allow Titian's burial near his masterpiece.

### ★ Top Tips

- No food is allowed in the church and picture-taking is discouraged. Appropriate dress is also required (eg no shorts, miniskirts or midriff- or tank-tops).
- Download a brochure of the basilica or grab a map at the ticket desk for a DIY tour of the incredible range of artworks.
- An audio guide (€2) is available in six languages.
- Atmospheric concerts are occasionally held in the church. Check the website for the schedule.

### Take a Break

For lunch seek out cosy Vineria all'Amarone (p107) for hearty plates of gnocchi and a range of Veneto wines.

Top Experience

# Shop for fresh food at Rialto Market

*Restaurants worldwide are catching on to a secret that this market has loudly touted for 700 years: food tastes better when it's seasonal and local. Before there was a bridge at the Rialto or palaces along the Grand Canal, there was a Pescaria (fish market) and a produce market. So loyal are locals to their market that talk of opening a larger, more convenient mainland fish market was swiftly crushed.*

MAP P96, G3

Rialto Mercato

041 296 06 58

Campo de la Pescaria

7am-2pm

Rialto Mercato

### Ponte di Rialto

A superb feat of engineering, Antonio da Ponte's 1592 Istrian stone span took three years and 250,000 gold ducats (about €19 million today) to construct. Adorned with stone reliefs depicting St Mark, St Theodore and the Annunciation, the bridge crosses the Grand Canal at its narrowest point, connecting the neighbourhoods of San Polo and San Marco.

### Pescaria

Slinging fresh fish for seven centuries and still going strong, the fishmongers of the **Pescaria** (Fish Market; Campo de la Pescaria; 7am-2pm Tue-Sun; Rialto Mercato) are more vital to Venetian cuisine than any chef. Starting at 7am, they sing the praises of today's catch: mountains of glistening *moscardini* (baby octopus), icebergs of inky *seppie* (cuttlefish) and buckets of crabs, from tiny *moeche* (soft-shell crabs) to *granseole* (spider crabs).

Sustainable fishing practices are not a new idea here; marble plaques show regulations set centuries ago for the minimum allowable sizes for lagoon fish. Seafood tagged 'Nostrana' is locally sourced, and the very best of it is sold at the stall of Marco Bergamasco, whose clients include Venice's Michelin-starred restaurants.

### Produce Market

Veneto *verdure* (vegetables) intrigue with their other-worldy forms, among them Sant'Erasmo *castraure* (baby artichokes), white Bassano asparagus and *radicchio di Treviso* (red, bitter chicory). In the winter, look out for prized *rosa di Gorizia,* a rose-shaped chicory specimen, often eaten raw with honey, vinegar and pancetta in its native region Friuli Venezia Giulia.

### ★ Top Tips

- Tuesday and Friday are the best market days; the Pescaria is closed on Monday.
- The fish stalls are all packed up by 2pm, but a few stalls usually linger on into the afternoon, selling produce, nuts, dried fruit and cooking oils.
- Locally sourced fish and produce is labelled 'Nostrana'.

### Take a Break

Join thirsty shoppers at cubby-hole Al Mercà (p106) for a chilled glass of Franciacorta.

After they pack up their stalls in the Pescaria, most fishmongers head to All'Arco (p102).

## Walking Tour

# Venice Culinary Adventure

*Before there were painters, opera divas or doges in Venice, there were fishmongers and grocers at the Rialto, bragging shamelessly about their wares. Today, the trade-route cuisine they inspired fills this corner of Venice with delectable discoveries for all your senses. Follow your growling stomach to find them on this culinary walking tour.*

**Start** Rialto Market; vaporetto Rialto Mercato

**Finish** Al Prosecco; vaporetto San Stae

**Length** 3.25km; two hours

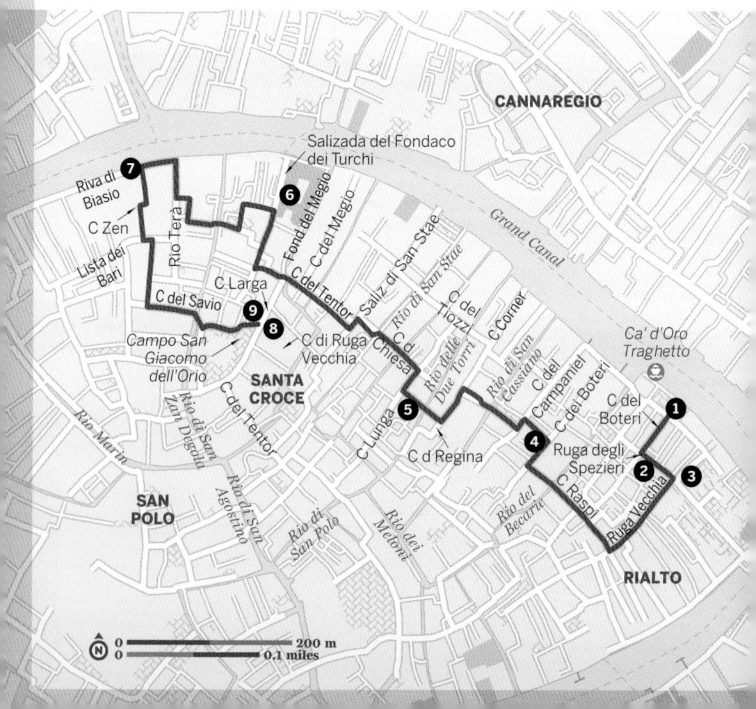

## ❶ Rialto Market

A trip through gourmet history starts at this **market** (p90), with its roofed Pescaria, where fishmongers artfully arrange the day's catch atop hillocks of ice.

## ❷ Drogheria Mascari

Glimpse trade-route treasures that made Venice's fortune at this gourmet **showcase** (p111). Spice pyramids grace shop windows, while specialty sweets are dispensed from copper-topped apothecary jars.

## ❸ Casa del Parmigiano

Displays of local San Daniele ham and Taleggio cheese at **Casa del Parmigiano** (p112) are reminders that Veneto's culinary fame wasn't built on seafood and spices alone.

## ❹ Veneziastampa

Cross a couple of bridges until you smell ink drying on letterpress menus and cookbook ex libris labels at **Veneziastampa** (p110).

## ❺ Museo di Storia Naturale di Venezia

Learn the scientific names of the lagoon creatures you spotted at the market at Venice's **museum of natural history** (p99), housed in a Grand Canal palace that was once the Turkish trading-house. It's filled with curious specimens, but architecture made from shellfish and fishbones steals the show.

## ❻ Riva di Biasio

Walk this sunny Grand Canal footpath allegedly named for 16th-century butcher Biagio (Biasio) Cargnio, whose sausages contained a special ingredient: children. When found out, Biasio was drawn and quartered.

## ❼ Gelato di Natura

Tradition meets innovation at this **gelato shop** (p104), which uses the finest DOP- and IGT-accredited local ingredients to make unusual small-batch flavours, along with vegan gelato and the East-meets-West *michi*, a Japanese rice cake with a gelato centre.

## ❽ Al Prosecco

Happy-hour temptations ring nearby Campo San Giacomo dell'Orio, but gourmet adventures deserve natural-process *prosecco* (sparkling wine) toasts at **Al Prosecco** (p105).

## ❾ Take a Break

Duck into **All'Arco** (p102) for the city's best *cicheti* (Venetian tapas) – ask for *una fantasia* (a fantasy), and father-son chefs Francesco and Matteo will invent a dish with ingredients you just saw at the market.

Walking Tour

# Fashion Finds in San Polo

*Treasure-hunt through San Polo artisan studios and design boutiques, and find your own signature Venetian style to stand out in any opening-night crowd. From one-of-a-kind paper jewels to custom velvet slippers, Venice's most original fashion statements ensure no one can steal your look – and usually cost less than global brands.*

**Start** Oh My Blue; vaporetto San Tomà

**Finish** Paperoowl; vaporetto San Stae

**Length** 2.3km; one hour

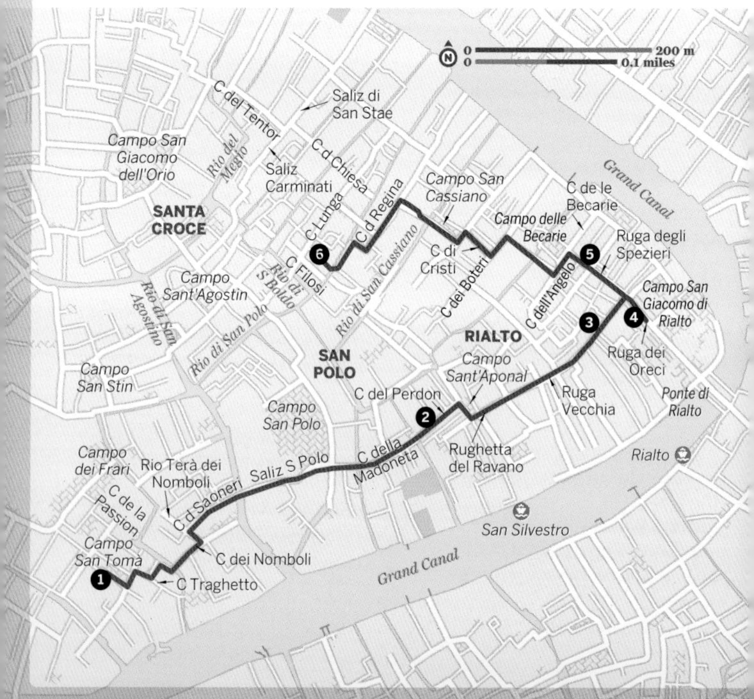

## ❶ Oh My Blue

Elena Rizzi's beautifully curated **gallery** (041 243 57 41; www.ohmyblue.it; Campo San Tomà 2865; 11am-1pm & 3.30-7.30pm; San Tomà) of contemporary art jewellery and homewares is worthy of a city hosting the most famous art fair in the world. Elena's Venetian eye for colour, form and texture results in a collection that feels uniquely Venetian.

## ❷ Damocle Edizioni

A meeting point for writers, artists and readers, **Damocle Edizioni** (346 8345720; www.edizionidamocle.com; Calle del Perdon 1311; 10am-1pm & 3-7pm Mon-Fri, 10am-1pm Sat; San Silvestro) is both a bijou bookshop and a publishing house, where Pierpaolo Pregnolato produces exquisite multilingual books. Emerging authors, out-of-print classics and rare unpublished works are his stock in trade.

## ❸ Alberto Sarria

One of the few traditional mask makers left in Venice, **Alberto Sarria** (041 520 72 78; www.masksvenice.com; Ruga Vecchia San Giovanni 777; 10am-7pm; San Stae) produces creations rendered in watercolour, acrylic and fine gilding, revealing the originality and subtle beauty of a master artisan. Alberto also makes delightful marionettes, featuring figures such as Arlecchino and the Bauta Uomo, two notorious characters from Venetian theatre.

## ❹ Pied à Terre

Venetian slippers stay sty colourful *furlane* (slipper **à Terre** (041 528 55 13; w piedaterre-venice.com; Sotoportego de Rialto 60; 10am-12.30pm & 2.30-7.30pm; Rialto Mercato). Handcrafted with recycled bicycle-tyre treads, they are ideal for finding your footing on a gondola. Choose from velvet, brocade or raw silk in vibrant shades of lemon and ruby. Don't see your size? Shoes can be custom-made and shipped.

## ❺ Maison 203

This fascinating **design company** (041 522 83 79; www.maison203.com; Ruga Vecchia San Giovanni 419; 10.30am-7pm; Rialto Mercato) produces jewellery and accessories in-store (as well as sourcing from designers around Europe), using materials such as bio-plastic and iron dust.

## ❻ Paperoowl

Stefania Giannici's nimble fingers have been practising origami since she was four years old. Now a master of her craft, she folds, prints, rolls, weaves and handpaints an extraordinary array of paper artworks at **Paperoowl** (041 476 19 74; www.paperoowl.com; Calle Longa 2155a; 10.30am-6pm Mon-Fri; San Stae). Must-haves include gorgeous Japanese-style decorative panels, delicate wind chimes inspired by the domes of Venetian churches and chic necklaces that look like Murano glass beads, but cost a fraction of the price.

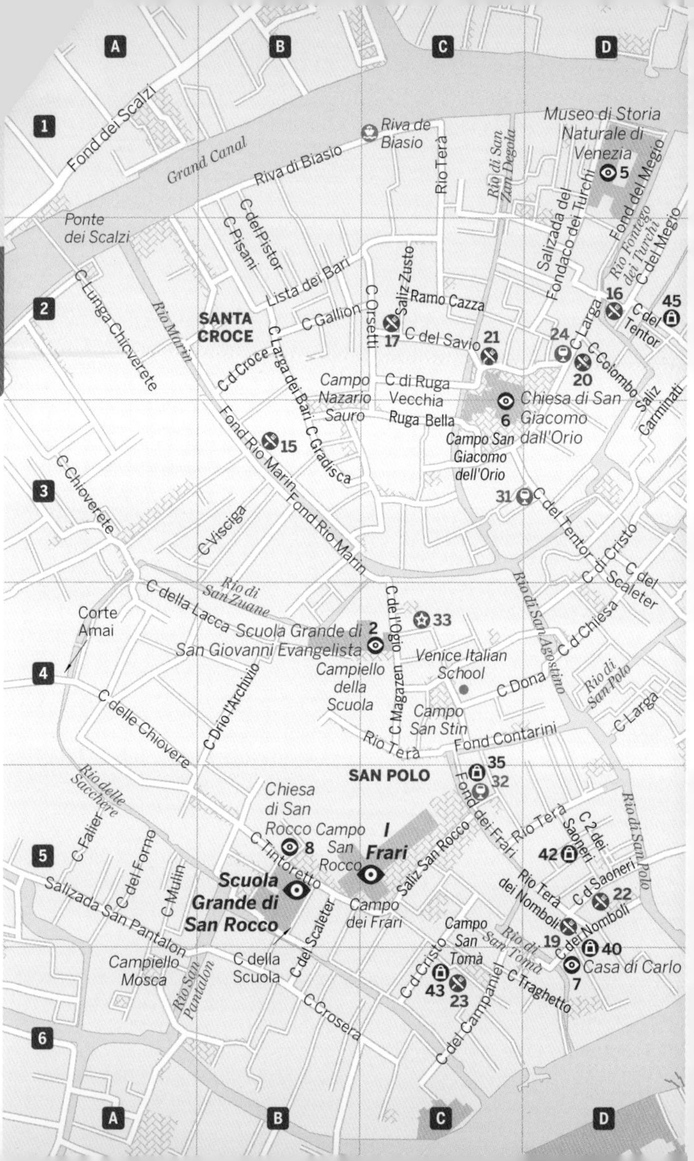
A
B
C
D
1
2
3
4
5
6
Fond dei Scalzi
Grand Canal
Riva de Biasio
Riva di Biasio
Rio Terà
Rio di San Zan Degola
Museo di Storia Naturale di Venezia
5
Salizada del Fondaco dei Turchi
Fond del Megio
Rio Fontego dei Turchi
C del Megio
Ponte dei Scalzi
C del Pistor
C Pisani
Lista dei Bari
Saliz Zusto
Ramo Cazza
C Lunga Chioverete
Rio Marin
SANTA CROCE
C Gallion
C Orsetti
17
C del Savio
21
24
C Larga
16
C del Tentor
45
C Colombo
20
C d Croce
C Larga dei Bari
Campo Nazario Sauro
C di Ruga Vecchia
Ruga Bella
Chiesa di San Giacomo dall'Orio
6
Saliz Carminati
Campo San Giacomo dell'Orio
Fond Rio Marin
15
C Gradisca
C Chioverete
31
C del Tentor
C Visciga
Fond Rio Marin
C di Cristo
C del Scaleter
Rio di San Zuane
C della Lacca
Scuola Grande di San Giovanni Evangelista
2
C de l'Ogio
33
Rio di San Agostino
Corte Amai
Venice Italian School
C d Chiesa
Campiello della Scuola
C Magazen
C Dona
Rio di San Polo
C Drio l'Archivio
C delle Chiovere
Campo San Stin
C Larga
Rio Terà
Fond Contarini
35
32
SAN POLO
Rio delle Sacchere
Chiesa di San Rocco
Campo San Rocco
I Frari
Fond dei Frari
Rio Terà
C 2 dei Saoneri
Rio di San Polo
C Falier
C del Forno
C Tintoretto
8
Saliz San Rocco
42
C Mulin
Scuola Grande di San Rocco
Salizada San Pantalon
C del Scaleter
Campo dei Frari
Rio Terà dei Nomboli
C d Saoneri
22
Campo San Tomà
Rio di San Tomà
19
C dei Nomboli
40
Campiello Mosca
C della Scuola
C d Cristo
43
23
C del Campaniel
C Traghetto
Casa di Carlo
7
Rio San Pantalon
C Crosera
C del Campaniel

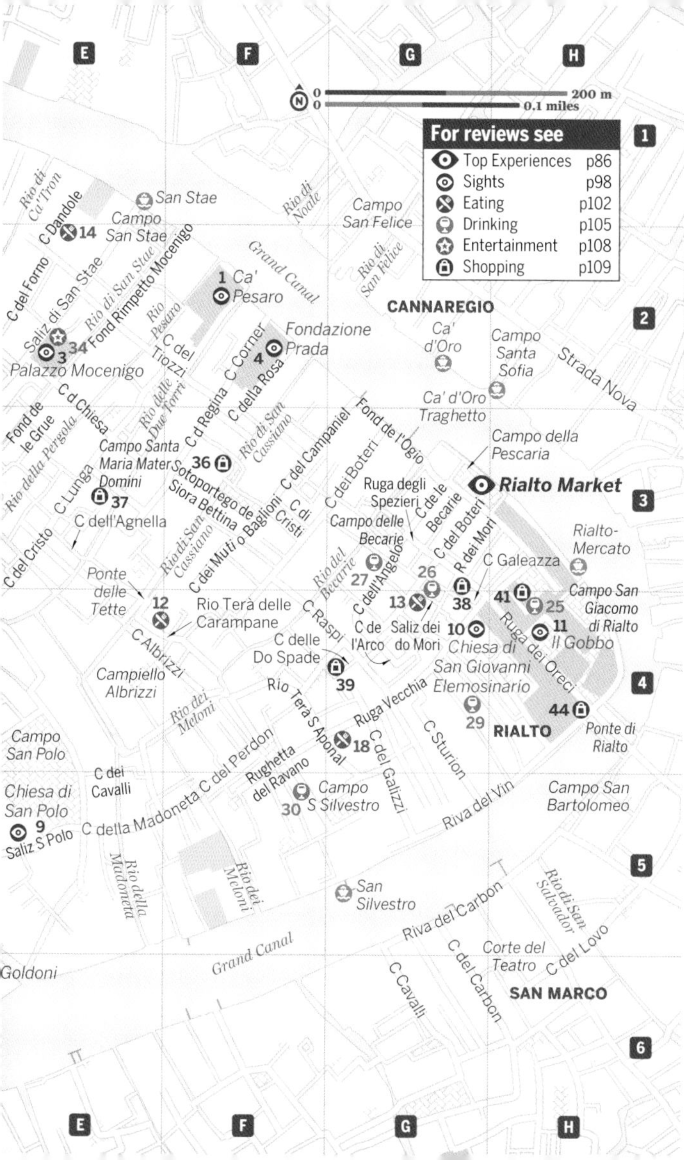
E
F
G
H
0 200 m
0 0.1 miles
For reviews see
Top Experiences p86
Sights p98
Eating p102
Drinking p105
Entertainment p108
Shopping p109
1
2
3
4
5
6
Rio di Ca' Tron
C Dandole
14
San Stae
Campo San Stae
Rio di Noale
Campo San Felice
Grand Canal
Rio di San Felice
C del Forno
Saliz di San Stae
Rio di San Stae
Fond Rimpetto Mocenigo
1 Ca' Pesaro
Rio Pesaro
CANNAREGIO
34
3
Palazzo Mocenigo
C del Tiozzi
C Corner
4
Fondazione Prada
Ca' d'Oro
Campo Santa Sofia
Strada Nova
C d Chiesa
Rio delle Due Torri
C della Rosa
Ca' d'Oro Traghetto
Fond de le Grue
Rio della Pergola
Campo Santa Maria Mater Domini
C d Regina
Rio di San Cassiano
C del Campaniel
Fond de l'Ogio
Campo della Pescaria
36
Sotoportego de Siora Bettina
C dei Boteri
Ruga degli Spezieri
C de le Becarie
Rialto Market
C Lunga
37
Rio della Pergola
C dell'Agnella
C dei Muti o Baglioni
C di Cristi
Campo delle Becarie
C del Boteri
R dei Mori
Rialto-Mercato
C del Cristo
Rio di San Cassiano
Rio del Becarie
C dell'Angelo
26
27
C Galeazza
Ponte delle Tette
12
Rio Terà delle Carampane
13
38
41
25
Campo San Giacomo di Rialto
C Raspi
C de l'Arco
Saliz dei do Mori
10
Chiesa di San Giovanni Elemosinario
Ruga dei Oreci
11
Il Gobbo
C Albrizzi
C delle Do Spade
39
Campiello Albrizzi
Rio Terà S Aponal
Ruga Vecchia
Rio dei Meloni
29
44
RIALTO
Ponte di Rialto
Campo San Polo
C del Perdon
18
C del Galizzi
C Sturion
Rughetta del Ravano
C dei Cavalli
Campo S Silvestro
30
Chiesa di San Polo
Riva del Vin
Campo San Bartolomeo
9
Saliz S Polo
C della Madoneta
Rio della Madoneta
Rio dei Meloni
San Silvestro
Rio di San Salvador
Riva del Carbon
Corte del Teatro
C del Lovo
Goldoni
Grand Canal
C Cavalli
C del Carbon
SAN MARCO
E
F
G
H

# Sights

## Ca' Pesaro

MUSEUM

1 MAP P96, F2

The stately exterior of this Baldassare Longhena–designed 1710 *palazzo* hides two intriguing art museums that could hardly be more different: the **Galleria Internazionale d'Arte Moderna** and the **Museo d'Arte Orientale**. While the former includes art showcased at La Biennale di Venezia, the latter holds treasures from Prince Enrico di Borbone's epic 1887–89 souvenir-shopping spree across Asia. Competing with the artworks are Ca' Pesaro's fabulous painted ceilings, which hint at the power and prestige of the Pesaro clan. (041 72 11 27; www.capesaro.visitmuve.it; Fondamenta de Ca' Pesaro 2076; adult/reduced €10/7.50, with Museum Pass free; 10am-5pm Tue-Sun; San Stae)

## Scuola Grande di San Giovanni Evangelista

HISTORIC BUILDING

2 MAP P96, C4

One of Venice's five main religious confraternities, the lay brothers of St John the Evangelist performed works of charity but also supported the arts by lavishing their clubrooms with treasures by the city's most famous painters and architects. Highlights include Pietro Lombardo's elaborately carved Renaissance **entry gate** (1481), topped with the eagle of St John; a Mauro Codussi–designed **staircase** (1498); and Giorgio Massari's spectacularly ostentatious **St John's Hall** (1727–62). (041 71 82 34; www.scuolasangiovanni.it; Campiello de la Scuola 2454; adult/reduced €10/8; 9.30am-5.15pm; San Tomà)

## Palazzo Mocenigo

MUSEUM

3 MAP P96, E2

Venice received a dazzling addition to its property portfolio in 1945 when Count Alvise Nicolò Mocenigo bequeathed his family's 17th-century *palazzo* to the city. While the ground floor hosts temporary exhibitions, the *piano nobile* (main floor) is where you'll find a dashing collection of historic fashion, including exquisitely embroidered men's silk waistcoats. Adding to the glamour and intrigue is an exhibition dedicated to the art of fragrance – an ode to Venice's 16th-century status as Europe's capital of perfume. (041 72 17 98; www.mocenigo.visitmuve.it; Salizada San Stae 1992; adult/reduced €8/5.50, with Museum Pass free; 10am-4pm; San Stae)

## Fondazione Prada

NOTABLE BUILDING

4 MAP P96, F2

This stately Grand Canal palace – designed by Domenico Rossi and completed in 1728 – has been commandeered by Fondazione Prada, which is renovating the palace. In between restoration work, Ca' Corner is the setting for slick temporary exhibitions of avant-garde art. If there isn't an exhibition scheduled, groups of six people or more can visit the palace free of charge between noon and 6pm on Friday. Bookings are required a week in advance. (Ca' Corner della Regina; 041 810 91 61; www.fondazioneprada.org; Calle de Ca' Corner 2215; San Stae)

## Museo di Storia Naturale di Venezia

MUSEUM

5 MAP P96, D1

Never mind the doge: insatiable curiosity rules Venice, and inside the former Fondaco dei Turchi (Turkish Trading House) it runs wild. The adventure begins upstairs with dinosaurs and prehistoric crocodiles, then dashes through evolution to Venice's great age of exploration, when adventurers such as Marco Polo fetched peculiar specimens from distant lands. There's also a courtyard and charming back garden, which is open during museum hours and ideal for picnics. (Natural History Museum of Venice; 041 275 02 06; www.msn.visitmuve.it; Salizada del Fontego dei Turchi 1730; adult/reduced €8/5.50, with Museum Pass free; 10am-6pm Tue-Sun; San Stae)

## Chiesa di San Giacomo dall'Orio

CHURCH

6 MAP P96, C2

Romanesque St James' Church was founded in the 9th century and completed in Latin-cross form in 1225, with chapels bubbling

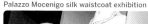

Palazzo Mocenigo silk waistcoat exhibition

UTA SCHOLL/SHUTTERSTOCK ©

along the edges. Within the serene gloom of the interior, notable artworks include luminous sacristy paintings by Palma Il Giovane, a rare Lorenzo Lotto *Madonna with Child and Saints* (1546), and an exceptional Paolo Veneziano crucifix (c 1350). (www.chorusvenezia.org; Campo San Giacomo da l'Orio 1457; adult/reduced €3/1.50, with Chorus Pass free; ⏲10.30am-4.30pm Mon-Sat; ⛴Riva de Biasio)

## Casa di Carlo Goldoni MUSEUM

7 MAP P96, D6

Venetian playwright Carlo Goldoni (1707–93) mastered second and third acts: he was a doctor's apprentice before switching to law, which proved handy when an *opera buffa* (comic opera) didn't sell. But as the 1st-floor display at his birthplace explains, Goldoni had the last laugh with his social satires. There's not really much to see here; the highlight is an 18th-century puppet theatre. (☎041 275 93 25; www.carlogoldoni.visitmuve.it; Calle dei Nomboli 2794; adult/reduced €5/3.50, with Museum Pass free; ⏲10am-4pm Thu-Tue; ⛴San Tomà)

## Chiesa di San Rocco CHURCH

8 MAP P96, B5

Built by Bartolomeo Bon between 1489 and 1508 to house the remains of its titular saint, beautiful St Roch's Church received a baroque facelift between 1765 and 1771, which included a grand portal flanked by Giovanni Marchiori statues. Bon's rose window was moved to the side of the church, near the architect's original side

Scuola Grande di San Rocco (p86)

door. On either side of the main altar are four vast paintings by Tintoretto depicting St Roch's life. The saint's casket is positioned above the altar. (041 523 48 64; www.scuolagrandesanrocco.org; Campo San Rocco 3053; adult/reduced €2/free; 9.30am-5.30pm; San Tomà)

### Chiesa di San Polo — CHURCH

9 MAP P96

Travellers pass modest St Paul's Church (founded in the 9th century) without guessing that major dramas unfold inside. Under the *carena di nave* (ship's keel) ceiling, Tintoretto's *Last Supper* (1569) shows apostles alarmed by Jesus' announcement that one of them will betray him. Giandomenico Tiepolo's *Way of the Cross* cycle in the Oratorio del Crocifisso (accessed from the rear of the church) shows onlookers tormenting an athletic Jesus, who leaps triumphantly from his tomb in the ceiling panel. (www.chorusvenezia.org; Campo San Polo 2118; adult/reduced €3/1.50, with Chorus Pass free; 10.30am-4.30pm Mon-Sat; San Tomà)

### Chiesa di San Giovanni Elemosinario — CHURCH

10 MAP P96, G4

Hunkering modestly behind T-shirt kiosks is this soaring brick church, built by Scarpagnino after a disastrous fire in 1514 destroyed much of the Rialto area. Cross the threshold to witness flashes of Renaissance genius: Titian's tender *St John the Almsgiver* (1545) altarpiece and gloriously restored dome frescoes of frolicking angels by Pordenone. (St John the Almsgiver's Church; www.chorusvenezia.org; Ruga Vecchia San Giovanni 478; €3, with Chorus Pass free; 10.30am-1.15pm Mon-Sat; Rialto Mercato)

### Venice's Saving Graces

While the Black Death ravaged the rest of Europe, Venice mounted an interfaith effort against the plague. The city dedicated a church and *scuola* (religious confraternity) to San Rocco where Venetians could pray for deliverance from the disease, while also consulting resident Jewish and Muslim doctors about prevention measures. Venice established the world's first quarantine zone, with inspections and 40-day waiting periods for incoming ships at Lazaretto. Venice's forward-thinking, inclusive approach created Scuola Grande di San Rocco's artistic masterpieces, which provide comfort to the afflicted and bereaved to this day, and set a public-health standard that has saved countless lives down the centuries.

### Il Gobbo — STATUE

11 MAP P96

Rubbed for luck for centuries, this renowned 1541 statue is now protected by an iron railing.

*Il Gobbo* (The Hunchback) served as a podium for official proclamations and punishments: those guilty of misdemeanours were forced to run a gauntlet of jeering citizens from Piazza San Marco to the Rialto. The minute they touched the statue their punishment was complete. (Campo San Giacomo di Rialto; Rialto Mercato)

## Eating

### Antiche Carampane VENETIAN €€€

12 MAP P96, E4

Hidden in the once shady lanes behind Ponte de le Tette, this culinary indulgence is hard to find but worth the effort. Once you do, say hello to a market-driven menu of Venetian classics, including *fegato alla veneziana* (veal liver with onions) and lots of seafood. It's never short of a smart, convivial crowd, so it's a good idea to book ahead. (041 524 01 65; www.antichecarampane.com; Rio Terà de le Carampane 1911; meals €55-63; 12.45-2.15pm & 7.30-10pm Tue-Sat; San Stae)

### All'Arco VENETIAN €

13 MAP P96, G3

Search out this authentic neighbourhood bar for some of the best *cicheti* (Venetian tapas) in town. Armed with ingredients from the nearby Rialto Market, father-son team Francesco and Matteo serve miniature masterpieces to the scrum of eager patrons crowding the counter and spilling out onto the street. Even with copious prosecco, hardly any meal here tops €20. (041 520 56 66; Calle de l'Ochialer 436; cicheti €2-2.50; 9am-2.30pm Mon-Sat; Rialto Mercato)

### Glam VENETIAN €€€

14 MAP P96, E2

Step out of your water taxi into the canalside garden of this inventive Michelin-starred restaurant in the Hotel Palazzo Venart. The contemporary menu focuses on local ingredients, pepping up Veneto favourites with unusual spices that would once have graced the tables of this trade-route city. The service and the wine list are equally impressive. (041 523 56 76; www.enricobartolini.net; Calle Tron 1961; meals €108-168; 12.30-2.30pm & 7.30-10.30pm; San Stae)

### Osteria Trefanti VENETIAN €€

15 MAP P96, B3

La Serenissima's spice trade lives on at simple, elegant Trefanti, where gnocchi might get an intriguing kick from cinnamon, and turbot is flavoured with almond and coconut. Seafood is the focus; try the 'doge's fettucine', with mussels, scampi and clams. Furnished with recycled copper lamps, the space is small and deservedly popular – so book ahead. (041 520 17 89; www.osteriatrefanti.it; Fondamenta del Rio Marin o dei Garzoti 888; meals €40-45; noon-2.30pm & 7-10.30pm Tue-Sun; ; Riva de Biasio)

## Osteria La Zucca

ITALIAN €€

16 MAP P96, D2

With its menu of seasonal vegetarian creations and classic meat dishes, this cosy, woody restaurant consistently hits the mark. Herbs and spices are used to great effect in dishes such as the nutmeg-tinged pumpkin and smoked ricotta flan. The small interior can get toasty, so reserve canalside seats in summer. Even in winter you're best to book ahead. (041 524 15 70; www.lazucca.it; Calle del Tentor 1762; meals €32-38; noon-2.30pm & 7-10.30pm Mon-Sat; ; San Stae)

## Trattoria Antica Besseta

VENETIAN €€€

17 MAP P96, C2

Wood panelling sets the scene at this veteran trattoria, known for giving contemporary verve to regional classics such as *bigoli in salsa* (wholemeal pasta with anchovies and onions), *saor* (onion marinade), seafood dishes and tiramisu. The dapper owner is a trained sommelier, a fact reflected in the inspired wine list. (041 72 16 87; www.anticabesseta.it; Salizada de Cà Zusto 1395; meals €40-52; 6.30-10pm Mon, Wed & Thu, noon-2pm & 6.30pm Fri-Sun; Riva de Biasio)

Italian gelato

DAVID REILLY/SHUTTERSTOCK ©

Venetian *cicheti*

## Ostaria dai Zemei

VENETIAN €

18 MAP P96, G4

Running this closet-sized *cicheti* counter are *zemei* (twins) Franco and Giovanni, who serve loyal regulars small bites with plenty of imagination: gorgonzola lavished with *peperoncino* (chilli) marmalade, duck breast drizzled with truffle oil, or chicory paired with leek and marinated anchovies. It's a gourmet bargain for inspired snacks and impeccable wines – try a crisp *nosiola* or invigorating prosecco brut. (041 520 85 96; www.ostariadaizemei.it; Rugheta del Ravano 1045; cicheti €2-5; 8.30am-8.30pm Mon-Sat, 9am-7pm Sun; San Silvestro)

## Bar Ai Nomboli

SANDWICHES €

19 MAP P96, D5

This snappy place is never short of local professors, labourers and clued-in out-of-towners. Crusty rolls are packed with local cheeses, fresh greens, roast vegetables, salami, prosciutto and roast beef, and served at an antique marble lunch counter. Beyond standard mayo, condiments range from spicy mustard to wild-nettle sauce and fig salsa. (041 523 09 95; Rio Terà dei Nomboli 2717c; sandwiches €2-6; 7am-9pm Sun-Fri, to 3pm Sat; ; San Tomà)

## Gelato di Natura

GELATO €

20 MAP P96, D2

Along with a dozen other things, Marco Polo is said to have introduced ice cream to Venice after his odyssey to China. At this gelato shop the experimentation continues with vegan versions of your favourite flavours, Japanese rice cakes and the creamiest, small-batch gelato incorporating accredited Italian ingredients such as Bronte pistachios, Piedmontese hazelnuts and Amalfi lemons. (340 2867178; www.gelatodinatura.com; Calle Larga 1628; 1 scoop €1.50; 10.30am-11pm Feb-Nov; ; Riva di Biasio, San Stae)

## Il Refolo

ITALIAN €€

21 MAP P96, C2

With outdoor tables occupying the *campo* in front of San Giacomo dall'Orio, this is a sunny spot from which to watch gondolas drift by. The food, too, is relaxed and unfussy with a menu offering a range of pizzas, pasta and light seafood dishes. Owned by the Martin family of Michelin-starred Da Fiore; expect top-quality ingredients and standout flavours. (041 524 00 16; www.facebook.com/Passito76; Campiello del Piovan 1459; pizzas €15, meals €35; noon-11pm Mar-Oct; ; Riva di Biasio)

### Trattoria da Ignazio VENETIAN €€

22 MAP P96, D5

Dapper white-jacketed waiters serve pristine grilled lagoon fish, fresh pasta and desserts made in-house ('of course') with a proud flourish, on tables bedecked with yellow linen. On cloudy days, homemade crab pasta with a bright Lugana white wine make a fine substitute for sunshine. On sunny days and warm nights, the neighbourhood converges beneath the garden's grape arbour. (041 523 48 52; www.trattoriadaignazio.com; Calle dei Saoneri 2749; meals €33-50; noon-3pm & 7-10pm Sun-Fri; San Tomà)

### Basegò VENETIAN €

23 MAP P96, C6

Focusing on three essential ingredients – good food, good wine and good music – this new-wave *cicheti* (Venetian tapas) bar has rapidly formed a faithful following. Indulge in a feast of lagoon seafood, prosciutto, smoked tuna, salami and cheese heaped on small slices of fresh bread. There's more seating than in most bars of this kind, and a dedicated kids' drawing area. (041 850 02 99; www.basego.it; Campo San Tomà 2863; cicheti €1.50-3; 10am-10pm; ; ; San Tomà)

### Talk, Eat, Live Italian

You see a rental sign on a palace door and you start daydreaming: morning banter with the greengrocer, lunchtime gossip at the local *bacaro* (bar), perhaps an evening *ti amo* at a canalside restaurant. There's no doubt that a grasp of Italian will enrich your experience of Venice and enhance your understanding of the city's culture. Luckily for you, **Venice Italian School** (Map p96; 347 9635113; www.veniceitalianschool.com; Campo San Stin 2504, San Polo; 1-/2-week group course €310/550, individual lessons €95; San Tomà) is run by Venetians Diego and Lucia Cattaneo, who offer excellent, immersive courses for adults and children between the ages of five and 13 years old.

## Drinking

### Al Prosecco WINE BAR

24 MAP P96, D2

Positioned on Venice's loveliest *campo* (square), this wine bar specialises in *vini naturali* (natural-process wines) – organic, biodynamic, wild-yeast fermented – from Italian winemakers. Order a glass of unfiltered 'cloudy' prosecco and toast the view over a plate of *cicheti* (Venetian tapas). (☎041 524 02 22; www.alprosecco.com; Campo San Giacomo da l'Orio 1503; ⏰10am-8pm Mon-Fri, to 5pm Sat; ⛴San Stae)

### Al Mercà

WINE BAR

25 MAP P96, H4

Discerning drinkers throng to this cupboard-sized counter on a Rialto Market square to sip on top-notch prosecco and other wines by the glass (from €2). Edibles usually include meatballs and mini *panini* (€1.50). (☎346 8340660; Campo Cesare Battisti già de la Bella Vienna 213; ⏰10am-2.30pm & 6-8pm Mon-Thu, to 9.30pm Fri & Sat; ⛴Rialto Mercato)

### Cantina Do Mori

WINE BAR

26 MAP P96, G4

You'll feel like you've stepped into a Rembrandt painting at venerable 'Two Moors', a dark, rustic bar with roots in the 15th century. Under gleaming, gargantuan copper pots, nostalgists swill one of around 40 wines by the glass, or slurp prosecco from old-school champagne coupes. Peckish? Bar bites include pickled onions with anchovies, succulent *polpette* (meatballs) and slices of *pecorino*. (☎041 522 54 01; Calle dei Do Mori 429; ⏰8am-7.30pm Mon-Fri, to 5pm Sat; ⛴Rialto Mercato)

### Cantina Do Spade

WINE BAR

27 MAP P96, G3

Famously mentioned in Casanova's memoirs, cosy 'Two Spades' was founded in 1488 and continues to keep Venice in good spirits with its bargain Tri-Veneto and Istrian wines and young, laid-back management. Come early for market-fresh *fritture* (fried battered seafood) and grilled squid, or linger longer with satisfying, sit-down dishes such as *bigoli in salsa* (pasta in anchovy and onion sauce). (☎041 521 05 83; www.cantinadospade.com; Sotoportego de le Do Spade 860; ⏰10am-3pm & 6-10pm Wed-Mon, 6-10pm Tue; 📶; ⛴Rialto Mercato)

### Bacareto da Lele

BAR

28 MAP P96, A4

Pocket-sized Da Lele is perpetually jammed with students and workers, stopping for a cheap, stand-up *ombra* (small glass of wine; from €0.70) on their way to and from the train station. Scan the blackboard for the day's wines and pair them with a little plate with salami, cheese and a roll (€1.60). It closes for much of August. (Campo dei Tolentini 183; ⏰6am-8pm Mon-Fri, to 2pm Sat; ⛴Piazzale Roma)

### Caffè del Doge

CAFE

29 MAP P96, G4

Sniff your way to the affable Doge, where dedicated drinkers slurp their way through the menu of speciality imported coffees, from

Ethiopian to Guatemalan, all roasted on the premises. If you're feel especially inspired, you can even pick up a stove-top coffee percolator. Pastries and viscous hot chocolate are on hand for those needing a sweet fix. (041 522 77 87; www.caffedeldoge.com; Calle dei Cinque 609; 7am-7pm; San Silvestro)

### Vineria all'Amarone — WINE BAR

30 MAP P96, F5

The warm wood-panelled interior and huge selection of Veneto wines by the glass are just part of the popularity of this friendly bar-cum-restaurant. Other reasons to stop by are generous *cicheti* platters, belly-warming plates of gnocchi and braised beef in red wine, and wine-tasting flights (€31 to €46), which include the heady Amarone from which the bar takes its name. (041 523 11 84; www.allamarone.com; Calle dei Sbianchesini 1131; 10am-11pm Thu-Tue; ; San Silvestro)

### Osteria da Filo — BAR

31 MAP P96, C3

A living room where drinks are served, this locals' hang-out comes complete with creaky sofas, free wi-fi, abandoned novels and the occasional live-music gig. Drinks are cheap and the Venetian tapas tasty. (Hosteria alla Poppa; 041 524 65 54; www.facebook.com/osteriadafilo; Calle del Tentor 1539; 4-11pm Mon-Fri, 11am-11pm Sat & Sun; ; Riva de Biasio)

Prosecco cocktails

### Grabbing Some Shade

The roots of Venetian bar culture date back at least to the 1700s, when Casanova was frequenting **Cantina Do Mori** (p106). The word *'bacaro'* derives from the name of the Roman wine god Bacchus, and the term *'ombra'* for a glass of wine has its own uniquely Venetian etymology. Whereas in most parts of Italy, *ombra* simply means 'shade' or 'shadow', its slang use in Venice dates back to the days when Venetian wine merchants would set up shop in the shadow of the San Marco bell tower, moving their wares throughout the day to stay out of the sun. In this context, *prendere un'ombra* – 'grab some shade' came to mean 'grab a glass of wine', an affectionate colloquialism that survives to this day.

### Il Mercante COCKTAIL BAR

32 MAP P96, C5

An hour's changeover is all it takes for historic **Caffè dei Frari** (041 476 73 05; Fondamenta dei Frari 2564; 9am-5pm; San Tomà) to transform itself into its night-time guise as Venice's best cocktail bar. If you can't find anything that takes your fancy on the adventurous themed cocktail list, the expert bar team will create something to suit your mood. In winter, snuggle on a velvet sofa upstairs. (041 476 73 05; www.ilmercantevenezia.com; Campo dei Frari 2564; 6pm-1am; San Tomà)

## Entertainment

### Palazetto Bru Zane CLASSICAL MUSIC

33 MAP P96, C4

Pleasure palaces don't get more romantic than this little *palazzo* on concert nights, when exquisite harmonies tickle Sebastiano Ricci angels tumbling across stucco-frosted ceilings. Multi-year restorations returned 17th-century Casino Zane's 100-seat music room to its original function, attracting world-class musicians to enjoy its acoustics. Free guided tours of the building run on Thursdays (in Italian/French/English at 2.30pm/3pm/3.30pm; none in August). (Centre du Musique Romantique Française; 041 521 10 05; www.bru-zane.com; Campiello del Forner o del Marangon 2368; adult/reduced €15/5; box office 2.30-5.30pm Mon-Fri; San Tomà)

### La Casa Del Cinema CINEMA

34 MAP P96, E2

Venice's public film archive shows original-language art films, including some in English, to members in a modern 50-seat, wood-beamed screening room inside Palazzo Mocenigo (p98). Check online for pre-release previews and revivals with introductions by directors, actors and scholars. (Videoteca Pasinetti; 041 274 71 40; www.comune.venezia.it; Salizada San Stae 1990; annual membership adult/reduced €35/25; 9am-1pm & 3-10pm Mon-Fri; San Stae)

bags constructed from re( advertising hoardings are the men's prison in Santa (041 524 31 25; www.riote pensieri.org; Fondamenta dei 2559a; 10am-8pm; San Tomà)

# Shopping

## Process Collettivo

GIFTS & SOUVENIRS

35 MAP P96, C5

A nonprofit cooperative runs this little shop, selling goods made by inmates of Venice's prisons as part of a social reintegration program. The toiletries are made from plants grown in the garden of the women's prison on Giudecca, while the very hip satchels and shoulder

## Artigianato d'Arte di Mauro Vianello

GLASS

36 MAP P96, F3

A coral reef's worth of painstakingly detailed glass Nemos, seahorses, starfish, jellyfish and seashells fills the window of this little glass studio. Alternatively you could opt for a biologically accurate reproduction of a delicate butterfly or a glistening snail. Book a demonstration if you want to watch the artist at work (adult/

Veneziastampa (p110)

## Venice's 'Honest Courtesans'

### The Age of Decadence

With trade revenues and the value of the Venetian ducat slipping in the 16th century, Venice's fleshpots brought in far too much valuable foreign currency to be outlawed. Instead, Venice opted for regulation and taxation. Rather than baring all in the rough-and-ready streets around the Rialto, prostitutes could only display their wares from the waist up in windows, or sit bare-legged on window sills. Venice decreed that to distinguish themselves from noblewomen who increasingly dressed like them, ladies of the night should ride in gondolas with red lights. By the end of the 16th century, the town was flush with some 12,000 registered prostitutes, creating a literal red-light district.

### Education Pays

Venice's *cortigiane oneste* were no ordinary strumpets. An 'honest courtesan' earned the title not by offering a fair price, but by providing added value with style and wit that reflected well on her patrons. They were not always beautiful or young, but *cortigiane oneste* were well educated, dazzling their admirers with poetry, music and apt social critiques. In the 16th century, some Venetian families spared no expense on their daughters' educations: beyond an advantageous marriage, educated women who become *cortigiane oneste* could command prices 60 times those of a *cortigiana di lume* ('courtesan of the lamp' – streetwalker).

### An Alternative Guidebook

A catalogue of 210 of Venice's *piu honorate cortigiane* (most honoured courtesans) was published in 1565, listing contact information and rates, payable directly to the courtesan's servant, her mother or, occasionally, her husband. A *cortigiana onesta* might circulate in Venetian society as the known mistress of one or more admirers, who compensated her for her company rather than services rendered. Syphilis was an occupational hazard, and special hospices were founded for infirm courtesans.

reduced €30/20). (041 520 18 02; www.maurovianello.com; Calle dei Morti 2251; 10.30am-6pm Mon-Sat; San Stae)

## Veneziastampa

ARTS & CRAFTS

37 MAP P96, E3

Mornings are best to catch the 1930s Heidelberg machine in

action, but whenever you arrive, you'll find mementos hot off the proverbial press. Veneziastampa recalls more elegant times, when postcards were gorgeously lithographed and Casanovas invited dates upstairs to 'look at my etchings'. Pick your signature symbols – meteors, faucets, trapeze artists – for original bookplates and cards. (041 71 54 55; www.veneziastampa.com; Campo Santa Maria Mater Domini 2173; 8.15am-7pm Mon-Fri, 9am-5pm Sat; San Stae)

## Drogheria Mascari FOOD & DRINKS

38 MAP P96, G3

Ziggurats of sun-dried tomatoes, leaning towers of star anise and chorus lines of olive oils draw awestruck foodies to Mascari's windows. Indoors, chefs clutch truffle jars like holy relics, kids ogle candy in copper-lidded jars and dazed gourmands grapple with aromatic honeys. For small-production Italian wines, don't miss the backroom cantina. (041 522 97 62; www.imascari.com; Ruga dei Spezieri 381; 8am-1pm & 4-7.30pm Mon, Tue & Thu-Sat, 8am-1pm Wed; Rialto Mercato)

## Gmeiner SHOES

39 MAP P96, G4

Gabriele Gmeiner honed her shoemaking craft at Hermès and John Lobb, and today jet-setters fly to Venice just for her ultra-sleek Oxfords with hidden 'bent' seams and her minutely hand-stiched brogues, made to measure for men and women (around €3000, including a hand-carved wooden

Meats and cheese in a Venice delicatessen

last). (☎338 8962189; www.gabrielegmeiner.com; Campiello del Sol 951; ⌚by appointment 8.30am-4pm Mon-Fri; ⛴Rialto Mercato)

## Sabbie e Nebbie

GIFTS & SOUVENIRS

40 MAP P96

East–West trade-route trends begin here, with chic cast-iron teapots, Japanese-textile patchwork totes, and Orient-inspired ceramics by Rina Menardi. Trained in design and graphics, owner Maria Teresa Laghi has a sharp eye for beautiful, unique and inspiring objects, making her shop especially popular with discerning locals. (☎041 71 90 73; www.sabbienebbie.com; Calle dei Nomboli 2768a; ⌚10am-12.30pm & 4-7pm Mon-Sat; ⛴San Tomà)

## Casa del Parmigiano

FOOD

41 MAP P96, H3

Suitably set beside the appetite-piquing Rialto Market, cheery Casa del Parmigiano heaves with coveted cheeses, from potent *parmigiano reggiano* (Parmesan) aged for three years, to rare, local Asiago Stravecchio di Malga. All are kept in good company by fragrant cured meats, *baccalà* (cod) and trays of marinated Sicilian olives. (☎041 520 65 25; https://casadelparmigiano.ve.it; Campo Cesare Battisti già de la Bella Vienna 214; ⌚8am-1.30pm Mon-Wed, to 7.30pm Thu-Sat; ⛴Rialto Mercato)

Hats for sale in a San Marco store

## Gilberto Penzo

ARTS & CRAFTS

42 MAP P96, D5

Yes, you actually can take a gondola home in your pocket. Anyone fascinated by the models at the Museo Storico Navale (p141) will go wild here, where you can shop for handmade wooden models of Venetian boats, including some that are seaworthy (or at least bathtub worthy). Signor Penzo also creates kits, so crafty types and kids can have a crack at it themselves. (041 71 93 72; www.veniceboats.com; Calle Seconda dei Saoneri 2681; 8.30am-1pm & 3-6pm Mon-Sat; San Tomà)

## Il Baule Blu

VINTAGE

43 MAP P96, C6

'The Blue Trunk' is a curiosity cabinet of elusive treasures where you can expect to stumble across anything from 1970s bubble sunglasses and antique Murano *murrine* (glass beads) to vintage Italian coats and frocks in good condition. (041 71 94 48; Campo San Tomà 2916a; 10.30am-12.30pm & 4-7.30pm Mon-Sat; San Tomà)

## Emilio Ceccato

CLOTHING

44 MAP P96, H4

If you've been eyeing up the natty striped T-shirts, devilishly soft winter wool hats and crepe pants sported by Venice's gondoliers then make a beeline for official supplier Emilio Ceccato. Here you'll find a huge selection of shirts, pants and jackets all emblazoned with the gondoliers supercool logo. What's more, proceeds from purchases are reinvested in training programs and boatyards. (041 522 27 00; www.emilioceccato.com; Sotoportego de Rialto 16-17; 10am-7pm; Rialto Mercato)

## Bottega Orafa ABC

JEWELLERY

45 MAP P96, D2

Master of metals, Andrea d'Agostino takes his influence from the Japanese technique of *mokume gane* (meaning 'metal with woodgrain'), masterful examples of which are on display in the Asian gallery of Ca' Pesaro (p98). The result is rings, pendants and bracelets with swirling multicoloured patterns that seem to capture the dappled lagoon waters for all time in silver and gold. (041 524 40 01; www.orafaabc.com; Calle del Tentor 1839; 9.30am-12.30pm & 3.30-7.30pm Tue-Sat; San Stae)

CORTE
SCALA MATA
1153

Explore

# Cannaregio & the Ghetto

*Anyone could adore Venice on looks alone, but in Cannaregio you'll fall for its personality. A few streets over from bustling Strada Nova is the Ghetto, a living monument to the outsized contributions of Venice's Jewish community. Between the art-filled Madonna dell'Orto and the Renaissance beauty of Santa Maria dei Miracoli are some of Venice's top cicheti (snack) bars and neighbourhood restaurants.*

## The Short List

- ***The Ghetto (p116)*** *Exploring the historic home/prison of Venice's centuries-old Jewish community.*
- ***Chiesa di Santa Maria dei Miracoli (p122)*** *Discovering this marble-clad church, a model of Venetian Renaissance architecture.*
- ***Chiesa della Madonna dell'Orto (p122)*** *Paying homage to Tintoretto at this, his local church and burial place.*
- ***Galleria Giorgio Franchetti alla Ca' d'Oro (p122)*** *Finding Grand Canal photo ops and misappropriated masterpieces at this glorious Gothic palazzo.*

## Getting There & Around

**Vaporetto** After Ferrovia stop, there are two more Grand Canal stops: San Marcuola (lines 1 and 2) and Ca' d'Oro (1). Lines 4.1, 4.2, 5.1 and 5.2 head from Ferrovia to Fondamente Nove. Line 3 goes to Murano. From Fondamente Nove, lines 12 and 13 head to the northern islands.

**Cannaregio & the Ghetto Map on p120**

**House in the Jewish Ghetto (p116)** LIZCOUGHLAN/SHUTTERSTOCK ©

Top Experience

# Explore Campo del Ghetto Nuovo & the Ghetto

*This Cannaregio corner once housed a getto (foundry), but its role as Venice's designated Jewish quarter from the 16th to 19th centuries gave the word a whole new meaning. From 1516 onwards, Jewish artisans and lenders tended to Venice's commercial enterprises by day, while at night and on Christian holidays they were restricted to the gated island of Ghetto Nuovo.*

MAP P120, D3

Guglie

### Museo Ebraico

At the Ghetto's heart, the **Museo Ebraico** (Jewish Museum; 041 71 53 59; www.museoebraico.it; Campo del Ghetto Nuovo 2902b; adult/reduced €8/6, incl tour €12/10; 10am-7pm Sun-Fri Jun-Sep, to 5.30pm Sun-Fri Oct-May; Guglie) explores the history of Venice's Jewish community through everyday artefacts, including finely wrought devotional objects and books published in the Ghetto during the Renaissance.

### The Synagogues

As you enter **Campo del Ghetto Nuovo** (pictured), look up: atop private apartments is the wooden cupola of the starkly beautiful 1575 **Schola Italiana** (Italian Synagogue; Campo del Ghetto Nuovo), the poorest Jewish community in the Ghetto.

Also recognisable from the square by its five long windows, the **Schola Tedesca** (German Synagogue; Campo del Ghetto Nuovo) has been the spiritual home of Venice's rich Ashkenazi community since 1528. The baroque pulpit and carved benches downstairs are topped by a gilded, elliptical women's gallery, modelled after a Venetian opera balcony.

In the corner of the *campo* is the wooden cupola of the **Schola Canton** (Corner Synagogue; Campo del Ghetto Nuovo), built c 1531 with gilded rococo interiors added in the 18th century.

Over the bridge in **Campo del Ghetto Vecchio**, Sephardic Jewish refugees raised two synagogues with 17th-century interiors attributed to Baldassare Longhena. **Schola Levantina** (Levantine Synagogue; Campo del Ghetto Vecchio) has a magnificent woodworked pulpit, while the **Schola Spagnola** (Spanish Synagogue; Campo del Ghetto Vecchio) has exuberant marble and carved-wood baroque interiors.

### ★ Top Tips

- Although you can stroll around this peaceful precinct day and night, the best way to truly experience the Ghetto is to take one of the guided synagogue tours offered by the Museo Ebraico, departing hourly from 10.30am.
- For information about local Jewish life, call into the **Jewish Community Info Point** (041 523 75 65; www.jvenice.org; Calle del Ghetto Vecchio 1222; 9.30am-5pm Mon-Fri).

### Take a Break

Ghetto Vecchio is home to one of Venice's best bakeries, Panificio Volpe Giovanni (p126), which serves speciality Jewish baked goods.

Indulge in a tasty, home-cooked lunch at family-run **Trattoria Pontini** (041 71 41 23; Fondamenta Cannaregio 1268; meals €20-25; 11.30am-10.30pm Mon-Sat; ; Guglie).

## Walking Tour

# Cannaregio's Cicheti Circuit

*After lavish canalside Cannaregio lunches, skip three-course dinners and make meals of cicheti (Venetian tapas) instead. Platters appear on counters across Cannaregio at 6pm, from perfect polpette (meatballs) to top-notch crudi (Venetian-style sashimi, laced with olive oil and/or aged balsamic vinegar). For bargain gourmet adventures, graze these Cannaregio cicheti hot spots.*

**Start** Al Parlamento; vaporetto Crea

**Finish** Un Mondo di Vino; vaporetto Rialto

**Length** 2km; one hour

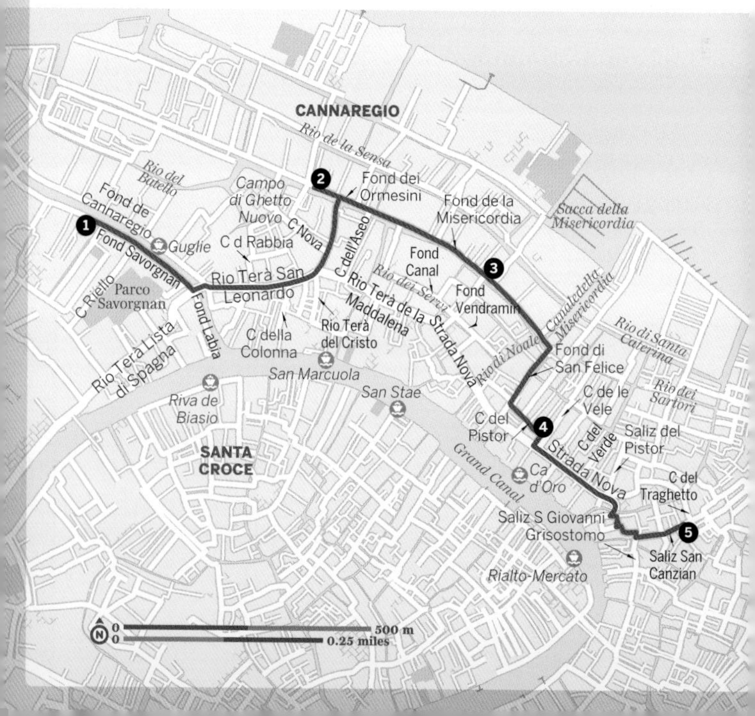

## ❶ Tramezzini & DJs at Al Parlamento

Entire university careers and international romances are owed to the powerful espresso, 6pm-to-9pm happy-hour cocktails and excellent overstuffed *tramezzini* (triangular stacked sandwiches) at **Al Parlamento** (☎041 244 02 14; www.facebook.com/alParlamento; Fondamenta Savorgnan 511; ⏰7.30am-2am; 📶; ⛴Crea). Draped ship ropes accentuate the canal views from the large windows at the front. Drop by in the evening and you might catch a live band or DJ set.

## ❷ Crostini & Concerts at Timon

Find a spot on the boat moored along the canal at **Timon** (☎041 524 60 66; www.altimon.it; Fondamenta dei Ormesini 2754; ⏰5pm-1am; ⛴San Marcuola) and watch the parade of drinkers and dreamers arrive for seafood *crostini* (open-face sandwiches) and quality organic and DOC wines by the *ombra* (half-glass) or carafe. Folk singers play sets canalside when the weather obliges; when it's cold, regulars scoot over to make room for newcomers at indoor tables.

## ❸ More Crostini at Vino Vero

Lining the exposed brick walls of **Vino Vero** (☎041 275 00 44; www.facebook.com/vinoverovenezia; Fondamenta de la Misericordia 2497; ⏰noon-midnight Tue-Sun, from 5pm Mon; ⛴San Marcuola) are interesting small-production wines, including a great selection of natural and biodynamic labels. However it's the *cicheti* that really lifts this place beyond the ordinary, with arguably the most mouth-watering display of continually replenished, fresh *crostini* in the entire city. In the evenings the crowd spills out onto the canal.

## ❹ Meatballs & Ombre at Osteria Alla Vedova

Culinary convictions run deep here at one of Venice's oldest **osterie** (☎041 528 53 24; Calle del Pistor 3912; meals €28-30; ⏰11.30am-2.30pm & 6.30-10.30pm Mon-Wed, Fri & Sat, 6.30-10.30pm Sun; ⛴Ca' d'Oro), so you won't find *spritz* (*prosecco* cocktails) or coffee on the menu or pay more than €2 to snack on a Venetian meatball. Enjoy superior seasonal *cicheti* and *ombre* with the local crowd at the bar, or call ahead for table service and strictly authentic Venetian dishes.

## ❺ Sarde in Saor at Un Mondo di Vino

Get here early for first crack at marinated artichokes and *sarde in saor* (sardines in tangy onion marinade) and claim a few square inches of ledge for your plate and wineglass. **Un Mondo di Vino** (☎041 521 10 93; www.unmondodivinovenezia.com; Salizada San Canzian 5984a; ⏰10am-midnight; ⛴Rialto) offers dozens of wines by the glass, so take a chance on a weird blend or obscure varietal.

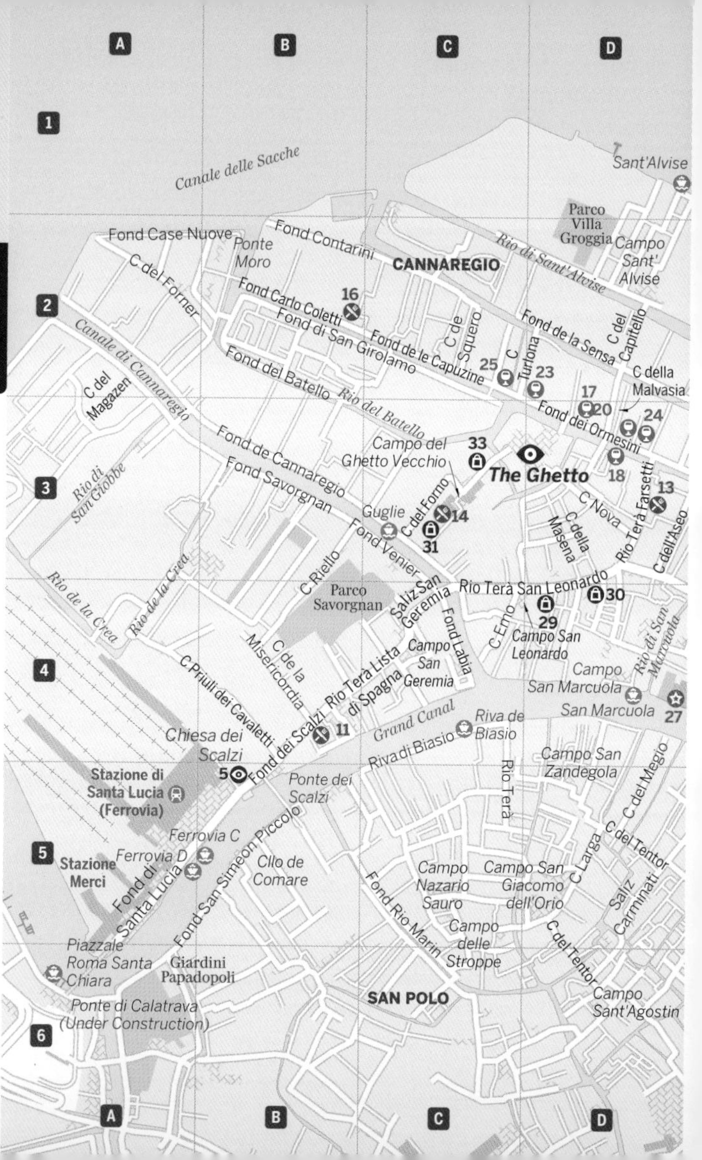

A
B
C
D
1
2
3
4
5
6
Canale delle Sacche
Sant'Alvise
Parco Villa Groggia
Campo Sant' Alvise
Rio di Sant'Alvise
Fond Case Nuove
Ponte Moro
Fond Contarini
CANNAREGIO
C del Forner
Fond Carlo Coletti
16
Fond di San Girolamo
Fond de le Capuzine
C de Squero
C Turlona
25
23
Fond de la Sensa
C del Capitello
C della Malvasia
17
20
24
Fond dei Ormesini
18
Canale di Cannaregio
C del Magazen
Fond del Batello
Rio del Batello
Campo del Ghetto Vecchio
33
The Ghetto
Fond de Cannaregio
Fond Savorgnan
Rio di San Giobbe
Guglie
C del Forno
14
31
C Nova
C della Masena
Rio Terà Farsetti
13
C dell'Aseo
Fond Venier
C Riello
Parco Savorgnan
Saliz San Geremia
Rio Terà San Leonardo
30
29
Fond Labia
C Emo
Campo San Leonardo
Rio di San Marcuola
Rio de la Crea
Rio de la Crea
C de la Misericordia
C Priuli dei Cavaletti
Rio Terà Lista di Spagna
Campo San Geremia
Campo San Marcuola
San Marcuola
27
Grand Canal
Riva de Biasio
Riva di Biasio
11
Chiesa dei Scalzi
Fond dei Scalzi
5
Stazione di Santa Lucia (Ferrovia)
Ponte dei Scalzi
Rio Terà
Campo San Zandegola
C del Megio
Ferrovia C
Ferrovia D
Stazione Merci
Fond di Santa Lucia
Fond San Simeon Piccolo
Cllo de Comare
Campo Nazario Sauro
Campo San Giacomo dell'Orio
C Larga
C del Tentor
Saliz Carminati
Fond Rio Marin
Campo delle Stroppe
C del Tentor
Piazzale Roma Santa Chiara
Giardini Papadopoli
SAN POLO
Campo Sant'Agostin
Ponte di Calatrava (Under Construction)

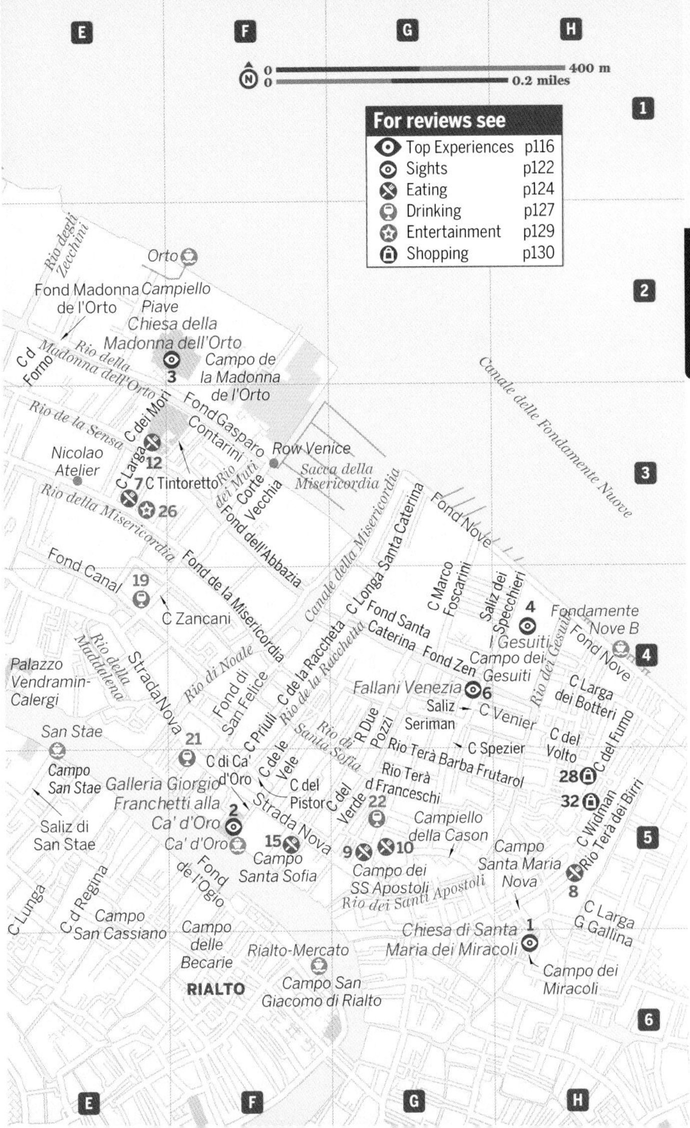

For reviews see
Top Experiences p116
Sights p122
Eating p124
Drinking p127
Entertainment p129
Shopping p130
400 m
0.2 miles
Orto
Fond Madonna de l'Orto
Campiello Piave
Chiesa della Madonna dell'Orto
Campo de la Madonna de l'Orto
Rio della Madonna dell'Orto
Rio de la Sensa
C dei Mori
Fond Gasparo Contarini
Row Venice
Sacca della Misericordia
Nicolao Atelier
C Larga
C Tintoretto
Rio dei Muti
Corte Vecchia
Rio della Misericordia
Fond dell'Abbazia
Canale della Misericordia
C Longa Santa Caterina
Fond Nove
Canale delle Fondamente Nuove
Fond Canal
C Zancani
Fond de la Misericordia
Fond Santa Caterina
C Marco Foscarini
Saliz dei Specchieri
Fondamente Nove B
Fond Nove
I Gesuiti
Campo dei Gesuiti
Fond Zen
Rio dei Gesuiti
Palazzo Vendramin-Calergi
Rio della Maddalena
Strada Nova
Rio di Noale
Fond di San Felice
C de la Racchetta
Rio de la Racchetta
Fallani Venezia
Saliz
C Venier
C Larga dei Botteri
Seriman
San Stae
Campo San Stae
Saliz di San Stae
C Priuli
Rio di Santa Sofia
R Due Pozzi
Rio Terà Barba Frutarol
C Spezier
C del Volto
C del Fumo
C di Ca' d'Oro
C de le Vele
C del Pistor
C del Verde
Rio Terà d Franceschi
Galleria Giorgio Franchetti alla Ca' d'Oro
Ca' d'Oro
Strada Nova
Campiello della Cason
C Widman
Rio Terà dei Birri
Campo Santa Sofia
Campo dei SS Apostoli
Campo Santa Maria Nova
Rio dei Santi Apostoli
Fond de l'Ogio
C Lunga
C d Regina
Campo San Cassiano
Campo delle Becarie
Rialto-Mercato
RIALTO
Campo San Giacomo di Rialto
Chiesa di Santa Maria dei Miracoli
Campo dei Miracoli
C Larga G Gallina
C d Forno
1
2
3
4
6
7
8
9
10
12
15
19
21
22
26
28
32
E
F
G
H

# Sights

## Chiesa di Santa Maria dei Miracoli
CHURCH

1 MAP P120, H6

This magnificent church was built between 1481 and 1489 to house Nicolò di Pietro's Madonna icon after the painting began to miraculously weep in its outdoor shrine. Aided by public fundraising, Pietro and Tullio Lombardo's design used marble scavenged from slag heaps in San Marco and favoured the human-scale of radically new Renaissance architecture in place of the grandiose Gothic status quo. (Campo dei Miracoli 6074; adult/reduced €3/1.50, with Chorus Pass free; 10.30am-4.30pm Mon-Sat; Fondamente Nove)

## Galleria Giorgio Franchetti alla Ca' d'Oro
MUSEUM

2 MAP P120, F5

One of the most beautiful buildings on the Grand Canal, with a lacy Gothic facade, 15th-century Ca' d'Oro is resplendent even without the original gold-leaf details that gave the palace its name (Golden House). Baron Franchetti (1865–1922) bequeathed this treasure-box palace to Venice, packed with his collection of masterpieces, many of which were originally plundered from Veneto churches during Napoleon's conquest of Italy. The baron's ashes are interred beneath an ancient purple porphyry column in the magnificent open-sided, mosaic-floored court downstairs. (041 522 23 49; www.cadoro.org; Calle di Ca' d'Oro 3932; adult/reduced €8.50/2; 8.15am-2pm Mon, to 7.15pm Tue-Sun, 2nd fl 10am-6pm Tue-Sun; Ca' d'Oro)

## Chiesa della Madonna dell'Orto
CHURCH

3 MAP P120, F2

This elegantly spare 1365 brick Gothic church remains one of Venice's best-kept secrets. It was the parish church of Venetian Renaissance painter Tintoretto (1518–94), who is buried in the chapel to the right of the altar. Inside, you'll find two of Tintoretto's finest works: *Presentation of the Virgin in the Temple* and *Last Judgment*, where lost souls attempt to hold back a teal tidal wave while an angel rescues one last person from the ultimate *acqua alta* (high tide). (www.madonnadellorto.org; Campo de la Madonna dell'Orto 3520; adult/reduced €3/2; 10am-5pm Mon-Sat; Orto)

## I Gesuiti
CHURCH

4 MAP P120, H4

Giddily over the top even by rococo standards, this glitzy 18th-century Jesuit church is difficult to take in all at once, with staggering white-and-green intarsia (inlaid marble) walls that look like a version of Venetian flocked wallpaper, marble curtains draped over the pulpit and a marble carpet spilling down the altar stairs. While the ceiling is a riot of gold-and-white stuccowork, gravity is provided by Titian's uncharacteristically gloomy *Martyrdom of St Lawrence*, on the left as you enter the church. (Santa Maria Assunta; ☎041 528 65 79; Salizada dei Specchieri 4882; €1; ⏰10.30am-1pm & 3.30-5pm; ⛴Fondamente Nove)

## Chiesa dei Scalzi

CHURCH

5 MAP P120 B5

An unexpected outburst of baroque extravagance, this Longhena-designed church (built 1654–80) has a facade by Giuseppe Sardi that ripples with columns and statues in niches. This is an unusual departure for Venice, where baroque ebullience was usually reserved for interiors of Renaissance-leaning buildings – in fact it was a deliberate echo of a style often employed in Rome, intended to help make the Discalced (meaning 'barefoot'; *scalzi* in Italian) Carmelites posted here from Rome feel more at home. (Chiesa di Santa Maria di Nazareth; ☎041 71 51 15; www.carmeloveneto.it; Fondamenta dei Scalzi 55-57; suggested donation €1; ⏰7.30-11.50am & 4-6.50pm; ⛴Ferrovia)

## Fallani Venezia

ARTS & CRAFTS

6 MAP P120, G4

Fiorenzo Fallani's laboratory has been credited with transforming screenprinting from a medium of reproduction to an innovative and creative artistic technique. Courses lead you from printing your own T-shirt through to more complex processes using different

Chiesa di Santa Maria dei Miracoli

colours, acetates and frames. Even if you don't fancy taking a course, this is a great place to purchase original art prints of Venice. (041 523 57 72; www.fallanivenezia.com; Salizada Seriman 4875; courses 1hr €40, 4hr €100-150, 8hr €200-300; Fondamente Nove)

## Eating

### Osteria da Rioba VENETIAN €€€

7 MAP P120, E3

Taking the lead with fresh seafood and herbs pulled from the family's Sant'Erasmo farm, Da Rioba's inventive kitchen turns out plates as colourful and creative as the artwork on the walls. This is prime date-night territory. In winter cosy up in the wood-beamed interior; in summer sit canalside. (041 524 43 79; www.darioba.com; Fondamenta de la Misericordia 2553; meals €46-49; 12.30-2.30pm & 7.30-10.30pm Tue-Sun; Orto)

### Osteria Boccadoro VENETIAN €€€

8 MAP P120, H5

The sweetly singing birds in this *campo* (square) are probably angling for your leftovers, but they don't stand a chance. Chef-owner Luciano and son Simone's creative *crudi* (raw seafood) are two-bite delights, and cloud-like gnocchi and homemade pasta are gone too soon. Fish is sourced from the lagoon or the Adriatic, and vegetables come from the garden. (041 521 10 21; www.boccadorovenezia.it; Campiello Widmann 5405a; meals €40-55; noon-3pm & 7-11pm Tue-Sun; Fondamente Nove)

### Ai Promessi Sposi VENETIAN €€

9 MAP P120, G5

Bantering Venetians thronging the bar are the only permanent fixtures at this neighbourhood *osteria* (casual tavern), where ever-changing menus feature fresh Venetian seafood and Veneto meats at excellent prices. Seasonal standouts include *seppie in umido* (cuttlefish in rich tomato sauce) and house-made pasta. (041 241 27 47; Calle d'Oca 4367; meals €30-40; noon-2.15pm & 6.30-10.15pm Tue-Sun, 6.30-10.15pm Mon; Ca' d'Oro)

### Trattoria da Bepi Già '54' VENETIAN €€

10 MAP P120, G5

Much better than it looks, Da Bepi is a traditional trattoria in the very best sense. The interior is a warm, wood-panelled cocoon, and service is efficient. Take their advice on the classic Venetian menu and order sweet, steamed spider crab, briny razor clams, grilled turbot with artichokes andn a tiramisu that doesn't disappoint. (041 528 50 31; www.dabepi.it; Campo SS Apostoli 4550; meals €25-35; noon-3pm & 7-10pm Fri-Wed; Ca' d'Oro)

### Pasticceria Dal Mas BAKERY €

11 MAP P120

This historic Venetian bakery-cafe sparkles with mirrors, marble and

## Venetian Jewish History

### Renaissance in the Ghetto

During the 14th- to 16th-century Italian Renaissance, pragmatic Venice granted Jewish communities the right to practise certain professions key to the city's livelihood, including medicine, trade, banking, fashion and publishing. Despite a 10-year censorship order issued by the Church in Rome in 1553, Jewish Venetian publishers contributed hundreds of titles popularising new Renaissance ideas on humanist philosophy, medicine and religion.

### Interfaith Enlightenment

Leading thinkers of all faiths flocked to Ghetto literary salons. In the 17th century, the Schola Italiana's learned rabbi Leon da Modena was so widely respected that Christians attended his services. When Venetian Jewish philosopher Sara Copia Sullam (1592–1641) was anonymously accused of denying the immortality of the soul – a heresy punishable by death under the Inquisition – Sullam responded with a treatise on immortality written in two days. The manifesto became a bestseller, and Sullam's writings are key works of early modern Italian literature.

### Signs of Restriction

On the wall at No 1131 Calle del Ghetto Vecchio, an official 1704 decree of the Republic forbids Jews converted to Christianity entry into the Ghetto, punishable by 'the rope [hanging], prison, galleys, flogging...and other greater punishments, depending on the judgment of their excellencies (the Executors Against Blasphemy)'. Such restrictions were abolished under Napoleon in 1797, when some 1626 Ghetto residents gained standing as Venetian citizens.

### The Enduring Legacy

Mussolini's 1938 Racial Laws revived discriminatory rules, and in 1943 most Jewish Venetians were deported to concentration camps. As a memorial on the northeast end of the Campo del Ghetto Nuovo notes, only 37 returned. Today few of Venice's 400-person Jewish community actually live in the Ghetto, but its legacy remains in bookshops, art galleries and religious institutions.

metal trim, fitting for the pastries displayed within. Despite the perpetual morning crush, the efficient team dispenses top-notch coffee and *cornetti* (Italian-style croissants) with admirable equanimity.

### Painting Venice

Sign up for a **Painting Venice** (340 5445227; www.paintingvenice.com; 2hr private lessons €100, 2-/4-day workshops €280/450) session with professionally trained and practising artists Caroline, Sebastien and Katrin and you'll strike out into tranquil *campi* (squares) in the tradition of classic Venetian *vedutisti* (outdoor artists). Beginners learn the basic concepts of painting 'en plein air', while those with more advanced skills receive tailormade tuition. It's a great way to slow down and really appreciate the colour and composition of each view.

Come mid-morning for mouth-watering, still-warm quiches. The hot chocolate is also exceptional. (041 71 51 01; www.dalmaspasticceria.it; Rio Terà Lista di Spagna 150; pastries €1.30-6.50; 7am-9pm; ; Ferrovia)

## Osteria L'Orto dei Mori

ITALIAN **€€€**

12 MAP P120, E3

Not since Tintoretto lived next door has this neighbourhood seen so much action, thanks to this bustling *osteria* (casual tavern). Sicilian chef Lorenzo makes fresh pasta daily, including squid atop *tagliolini*. Fish-shaped lamps set a playful mood in an upmarket space. (041 524 36 77; www.osteriaortodeimori.com; Campo dei Mori 3386; meals €45-50; 12.30-3pm & 7-11pm Wed-Mon; Orto)

## Cantina Aziende Agricole

VENETIAN **€**

13 MAP P120, D3

This friendly hole-in-the-wall *bacaro* (bar) serves an impressive array of local wine to a loyal group of customers who treat the place much like a social club. Join them for a glass of Raboso and heaped platters of *lardo* (cured pork fat), cheese drizzled with honey, *polpette* (meatballs) and deep-fried pumpkin fritters. (333 3458811; www.cantinaaziendeagricole.com; Rio Terà Farsetti 1847a; meals €12, cicheti €1.50-1.80; 9am-2pm & 5-10pm; San Marcuola)

## Panificio Volpe Giovanni

BAKERY **€**

14 MAP P120, C3

In addition to unleavened pumpkin and radicchio bread, this kosher bakery sells unusual treats such as crumbly *impade* (biscuity logs flavoured with ground almonds) and *orecchiette di Amman* ('little ears of Amman'; ear-shaped pastries stuffed with chocolate), along with quite possibly the best *cornetti* (Italian-style croissants) in Venice. (041 71 51 78; www.facebook.com/PanificioVolpeGiovanni; Calle del Ghetto Vecchio 1143; pastries €1.50-3; 7am-7.30pm Mon-Sat, 8.30am-1pm Sun; Guglie)

### Gelateria Ca' d'Oro

GELATO €

15 MAP P120, F5

Foot traffic stops here for spectacularly creamy gelato made in-house daily. For a summer pick-me-up, try the *granita di caffe con panna* (coffee shaved ice with whipped cream). (041 522 89 82; Strada Nova 4273b; scoops €1.80; 10.30am-10pm; Ca' d'Oro)

### Alle Due Gondolette

VENETIAN €€

16 MAP P120, B2

On Fridays it's worth walking the extra mile to this working-class diner for its generous servings of *baccalà* (cod), either creamed with olive oil, lemon and parsley or *alla Vicentina* (braised with onions, anchovies and milk). Other classics on the menu include pasta with octopus, peas and mint, and gnocchi with chicken and *pecorino*. (041 71 75 23; www.alleduegondolette.com; Fondamente de le Capuzine 3016; meals €25-35; 12.15-2.30pm & 7-10pm Mon-Sat; Tre Archi)

## Drinking

### Birreria Zanon

BAR

17 MAP P120, D3

There's something of a mini beer craze developing along Fondamente dei Ormesini, and Birreria Zanon is the latest contender, wooing customers with its sunny setting, laid-back vibe and huge craft-beer selection. Particularly tasty are the *tramezzini* (triangular, stacked sandwiches) on black bread, which go down a treat

Casinò Di Venezia (p130)

## High Tides

*Acqua alta* (high water) isn't an emergency – it's a tide reaching 110cm above normal levels and normally happens four to six times a year, between November and April. *Acqua alta* may cause flooding in low-lying areas, but waters usually recede within five hours.

To see if *acqua alta* is likely, check Venice's Centro Maree 48-hour tidal forecast at www.comune.venezia.it. Alarms sound when *acqua alta* is expected to reach the city within two to four hours:

- One even tone (up to 110cm above normal): Barely warrants pauses in happy-hour conversation.
- Two rising tones (110cm to 120cm): You might need *stivali di gomma* (rubber boots).
- Three rising tones (around 130cm): Check Centro Maree online to see where *passarelle* (gangplank walkways) are in use.
- Four rising tones (140cm and up): Businesses may close early.

with a pint of Grimbergen amber ale. (041 476 23 47; Fondamenta dei Ormesini 2735; 9am-10pm; Guglie)

### Marciano Pub

PUB

18 MAP P120, D3

With its wooden bar and gleaming brass beer taps, this Anglo-Venetian hostelry certainly looks authentic. Marciano takes booze seriously, stocking craft beers from around the globe, including its own brew and samphire-infused gin. The same goes for the food menu of sustainably sourced burgers (€12 to €16) and steaks, including kangaroo and ostrich. (041 47 62 55; www.facebook.com/marcianopubvenezia; Calle Gheltof o Loredan 1863c; 5pm-1am Fri-Wed; San Marcuola)

### Il Santo Bevitore

PUB

19 MAP P120, E4

San Marco has its glittering cathedral, but beer lovers prefer pilgrimages to this shrine of the 'Holy Drinker' for 20 brews on tap, including Trappist ales and seasonal stouts. There's also a big range of speciality gin, whisky and vodka. (335 8415771; www.ilsantobevitorepub.com; Calle Zancani 2393a; 4pm-2am; ; Ca' d'Oro)

### Torrefazione Cannaregio

CAFE

20 MAP P120, C3

The only micro-roastery in Venice, this brick-lined cafe perched on a sunny canal bank is filled with house-made roasts including the flagship Remer, an Arabica blend with a smooth, chocolate aftertaste. For those who like more punch there are Robusta blends, plus some delightful speciality teas. The Marchi family has been roasting since the 1930s. (041 71 63 71; www.torrefazionecannaregio.it; Fondamenta dei Ormesini 2804; 7am-7.30pm Mon-Sat, 9am-6pm Sun; Guglie)

### La Cantina WINE BAR

21 MAP P120, F5

While you can sit down out the back for a serious seafood feast, we prefer to sample the wine and *cicheti* (Venetian tapas) selection while propped up at the bar or on the square at one of the tables fashioned from old wine barrels. (041 522 82 58; Campo San Felice 3689; 11am-11pm; Ca' d'Oro)

### El Sbarlefo BAR

22 MAP P120, G5

All sorts sidle into this attractive little *cicheti* bar, from local hipsters to candidates for hip replacements, drawn by an excellent wine selection and a tasty array of snacks. (041 523 30 84; www.elsbarlefo.it; Salizada del Pistor 4556c; 10am-11pm; ; Ca' d'Oro)

### Dodo Caffè BAR

23 MAP P120, D2

For sunsets as rosy as your *Aperol spritz*, arrive early to snag canalside seating at this local favourite. The Dodo crew offers a warm welcome to strangers, along with generously stuffed *panini* and *tramezzini* (triangular, stacked sandwiches). (041 71 59 05; www.facebook.com/DodoCaffe; Fondamenta dei Ormesini 2845; 8.15am-midnight; San Marcuola)

### Birre da Tutto il Mondo o Quasi BAR

24 MAP P120, D3

While the rest of Venice is awash in wine, 'Beers from Around the World or Almost' offers more than 100 brews, including reasonably priced bottles of craft ales and local Birra Venezia. (041 71 58 34; Fondamenta dei Ormesini 2710; 11am-4pm & 6pm-2am Mon-Sat; Orto)

### Bagatela BAR

25 MAP P120, C2

An unpretentious, popular late-night hang-out crammed with Cannaregio locals, indie rockers and students, Bagatela offers bottled beers, cocktails, board games, sports on the TV and a rather disconcerting skull behind the bar. (328 7255782; www.bagatelavenezia.com; Fondamente de le Capuzine 2925; 6pm-1am Wed-Sun; Guglie)

## Entertainment

### Paradiso Perduto LIVE MUSIC

26 MAP P120, E3

'Paradise Lost' is a find for anyone craving a cold beer canalside on a hot summer's night. Although the restaurant is also popular, the Paradiso is particularly noted for

### Adventures in Wine & Cicheti

*Prosecco*, Soave and Amarone aren't the only wines in town. Expand your happy-hour options on a unique Cichetto Row with **Row Venice** (Map p120; ☎347 7250637; www.rowvenice.org; Fondamenta Contarini; 90min lessons per 1-2 people €85, 3/4 people 120/140; ⛴Orto). This gentle 2½-hour row bar-hops between Cannaregio's canalside bars (€240 for two people) with handy instructions on Veneto varieties and *voga* (Venetian rowing). The outfit also offers half-hour lessons (from €85) on rowing a traditional *batellina coda di gambero* (shrimp-tailed boat) standing up like gondoliers do.

Landlubbers in search of a good backstreet *bacaro* (bar) crawl, should opt for fun and informed tours with Monica Cesarato from **Cook in Venice** (www.cookinvenice.com; tours €40-60, courses €150-350).

its Monday-night gigs; Chet Baker, Keith Richards and Vinicio Capossela have all played the small stage. (☎041 72 05 81; Fondamenta de la Misericordia 2540; 🕓11am-1am Thu-Mon; ⛴Orto)

### Casinò Di Venezia — CASINO

27 MAP P120, D4

Founded in 1638, the world's oldest casino moved into its current palatial home in the 1950s. Slots open at 11am; arrive after 3.30pm wearing your jacket and poker face for gaming tables. Arrive in style with a free water-taxi ride from Piazzale Roma. (Ca' Vendramin Calergi; ☎041 529 71 11; www.casinovenezia.it; Calle Vendramin 2040; admission incl gaming token €10; 🕓11am-2.45am Sun-Fri, to 3.15am on Sat; ⛴San Marcuola)

## Shopping

### Gianni Basso — STATIONERY

28 MAP P120, H5

Gianni Basso doesn't advertise his letterpressing services: the calling cards crowding his workshop window do the trick. From Microsoft COO's to celebrities and royalty, movers and shakers from around the world get their business cards, invitations and stationery printed here. Trained at the Armenian Monastery, Gianni is as much a piece of Venetian history as his miniature print museum next door. (☎041 523 46 81; Calle del Fumo 5306; 🕓9am-1pm & 2-6pm Mon-Fri, 9am-noon Sat; ⛴Fondamente Nove)

### Balducci Borse — SHOES

29 MAP P120, D4

Venice isn't known for its leatherwork, but there's always an exception to the rule – and Franco Balducci is it. Step through the door of his Cannaregio workshop and you can smell the quality of the hand-picked Tuscan hides that he fashions on the premises into glossy shoulder bags and women's boots. (041 524 62 33; www.balducciborse.com; Rio Terà San Leonardo 1593; 9.30am-1pm & 2.30-7.30pm; San Marcuola)

### Leonardo
JEWELLERY

30 MAP P120, D4

Hiding in plain sight on touristy Strada Nova, this authentic Murano glass shop stocks jewellery from some of Venice's very best glass artists, many of whom rarely sell outside their own showrooms. (041 524 43 07; Rio Terà San Leonardo 1703; 10am-8pm; San Marcuola)

### Antichità al Ghetto
ANTIQUES

31 MAP P120, C3

Instead of a souvenir T-shirt, how about taking home a memento of Venetian history: an ancient map of the canal, an etching of Venetian dandies daintily alighting from gondolas or an 18th-century cameo once worn by the most fashionable ladies in the Ghetto. (041 524 45 92; www.antichitaalghetto.com; Calle del Ghetto Vecchio 1133/4; 10am-7pm; Guglie)

### Vittorio Costantini
GLASS

32 MAP P120, H5

Kids and adults alike are thrilled at the magical, miniature insects, butterflies, shells and birds that Vittorio Costantini fashions out of glass using a lampwork technique. (041 522 22 65; www.vittoriocostantini.com; Calle del Fumo 5311; 9.30am-1pm & 2.15-5.30pm Mon-Fri; Fondamente Nove)

### Dressing for Carnevale

If you're wondering where Cinderella goes to find the perfect ball gown for Carnevale or Prince Charming his tights, look no further than **Nicolao Atelier** (Map p120; 041 520 70 51; www.nicolao.com; Fondamenta de la Misericordia 2590; 9.30am-1pm & 2-6pm Mon-Fri; San Marcuola). In his past life, Stefano Nicolao was an actor and an assistant costumier before finding his true calling as a scholar and curator of historical fashion, over 10,000 pieces of which are now stored in his vast studio. An exquisite handmade Carnevale outfit will set you back €250 to €300.

### La Stamperia del Ghetto
ARTS & CRAFTS

33 MAP P120, C3

Keep your eyes peeled for Enzo Aboaf's wonderful Ghetto gallery filled with rare original copperplate prints and etchings of the Ghetto and Venice. In among them is a stash of Emanuele 'Lele' Luzzati's highly collectible Chagall-style illustrations. (041 275 02 00; Calle del Ghetto Vecchio 1185a; 10am-4pm Sun-Fri; Guglie)

# Explore Castello

*Stretching eastwards from San Marco, Castello is the city's largest neighbourhood, containing the Arsenale shipyards where Venetian craftsmen made seafaring history, alongside Gothic, Byzantine and Dalmation churches, frescoed orphanages where Vivaldi conducted and avant-garde Biennale pavilions. At the tip of Venice's tail is a pine-shaded park where Venetians go to rest, play and get away.*

## The Short List

- ***Riva degli Schiavoni (p135)*** *Taking a stroll along Castello's picturesque waterfront promenade.*
- ***Zanipolo (p138)*** *Gawking at the scale of this 14th-century church and admiring its artistic masterworks.*
- ***Palazzo Grimani (p139)*** *Viewing classical statuary in this theatrical Renaissance palazzo.*
- **La Biennale di Venezia *(p140)*** *Pondering modern art and ground-breaking architecture in the Arsenale and Giardini Pubblici.*
- ***Scuola Dalmata di San Giorgio degli Schiavoni (p138)*** *Basking in the golden glow of Carpaccio's paintings in this Dalmatian confraternity house.*

## Getting There & Around

**Vaporetto** Castello is encircled with vaporetto stops. Lines 4.1 and 4.2 stop at all of them as they loop around the perimeter of Venice; similarly 5.1 and 5.2 stop at all but Arsenale. Line 1 makes all the southern stops, linking them to the Grand Canal and the Lido. The busiest stop is San Zaccaria (also called San Marco San Zaccaria), with multiple jetties spread along Riva degli Schiavoni.

**Castello Map on p136**

Arsenale shipyard (p141) DIMBAR76/SHUTTERSTOCK ©

## Walking Tour

# Castello's Byways

*Leave the crowds and cramped quarters of San Marco behind, and stretch your legs on a sunny stroll through Castello, where saints and sailors come with the territory.*

**Start** Zanipolo (Chiesa di SS Giovanni e Paolo); vaporetto Ospedale

**Finish** Giardini Pubblici; vaporetto Giardini

**Length** 6.5km; three hours

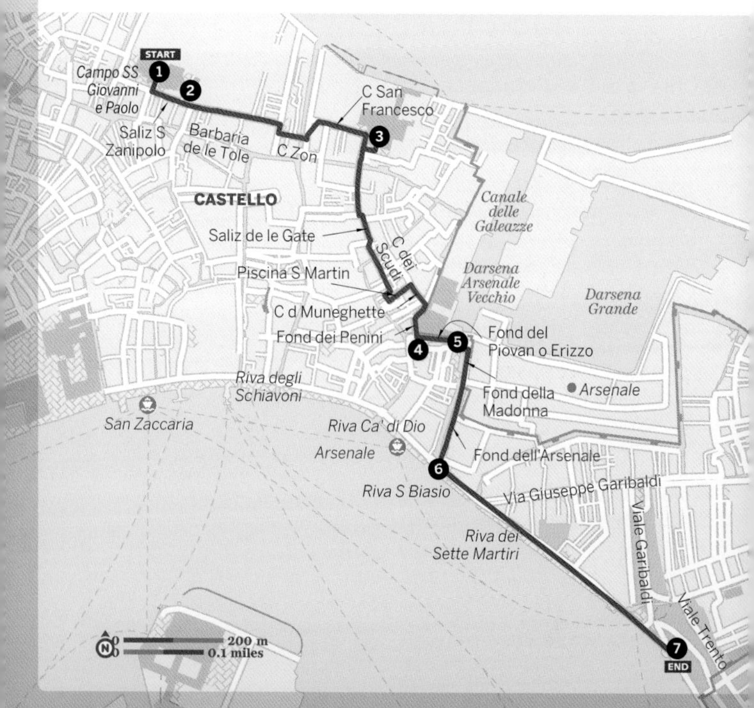

## ❶ Zanipolo

Rising above Castello's tallest ship-masts is Gothic **Zanipolo** (p138) basilica. Its 33m-high nave provides a fitting setting for 25 doges' tombs.

## ❷ Ospedaletto

A block east, you can't miss statue-bedecked **Ospedaletto** (Chiesa di Santa Maria dei Derelitti; ☎041 309 66 05; www.gioiellinascostidivenezia.it; Barbaria de le Tole 6691; ⏰by reservation; ⛴Ospedale), a 1660s orphanage designed by Longhena. This refuge was once famed for its orchestra of orphan girls.

## ❸ Chiesa di San Francesco della Vigna

Continue down Barbaria delle Tole, then dog-leg left to see Palladio-colonnaded **Chiesa di San Francesco della Vigna** (p138), where Antonio Negroponte's Madonna and child float like a hovercraft above Venice's lagoon.

## ❹ Chiesa di San Martino

Heading south, you'll bump into the massive walls of the **Arsenale** (p141), Venice's legendary shipyard. Turn right at Campo de le Gorne and follow the walls to this **church** (Campo San Martino 2298; admission free; ⏰9.15am-11.45 & 3.30-6pm Mon-Sat, to 5.30pm Sun; ⛴Arsenale) dedicated to St Martin, patron saint of wine and soldiers. By the doorway is a *bocca di leoni* (mouth of the lion), a slot where Venetians slipped denunciations of their neighbours. *Arsenalotti* (Arsenale workers) were sworn to silence about trade secrets, since loose lips could sink ships.

## ❺ Porta Magna

The Arsenale's main gate is considered the city's earliest Renaissance structure. By the 18th century naval production at the Arsenale had dwindled and the republic was in terminal decline. In 1797 La Serenissima surrendered to Napoleon without a fight.

## ❻ Riva

From **Riva degli Schiavoni** (⛴San Zaccaria) turn south onto Castello's breathtaking waterfront promenade to admire sweeping views across the lagoon.

## ❼ Giardini Pubblici

The Napoleonic **public gardens** (p138) are dotted with Biennale pavilions, thronged summer through fall with artists, architects and admirers from around the world. Between Biennales you can still enjoy the rest of the park.

### Take a Break

After your walk, enjoy a heavenly herbal tisane inside Napoleon's greenhouse at **Serra dei Giardini** (p146) – or a sailor-size *spritz* (*prosecco* cocktail) and lagoon-front seat at **Paradiso** (☎041 241 39 72; www.inparadiso.net; Giardini Pubblici 1260; ⏰9am-9pm; ⛴Giardini Biennale).

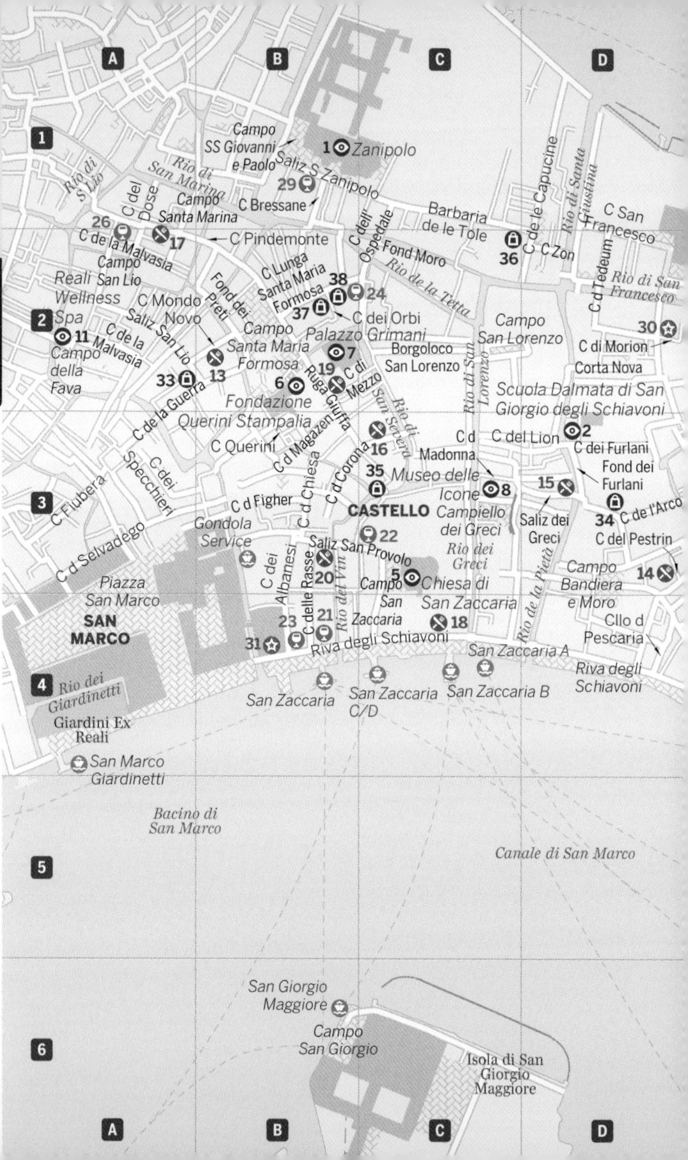
A
B
C
D
1
2
3
4
5
6
Campo SS Giovanni e Paolo
1 Zanipolo
Saliz S Zanipolo
29
Rio di S Lio
Rio di San Marina
Campo Santa Marina
C del Dose
C Bressane
26
17
C Pindemonte
C de la Malvasia
Campo Reali San Lio
Wellness Spa
11
C Mondo Novo
Saliz San Lio
C de la Malvasia
Campo della Fava
Fond dei Preti
C Lunga Santa Maria Formosa
38
24
37
C dei Orbi
Campo Santa Maria Formosa
13
33
Palazzo Grimani
7
19
C di Mezzo
Ruga Giuffa
6
Fondazione Querini Stampalia
C de la Guerra
C Querini
C d Magazen
C dell' Ospedale
Barbaria de le Tole
Fond Moro
Rio de la Tetta
36
C de le Capucine
C Zon
Rio di Santa Giustina
C San Francesco
C d Tedeum
Rio di San Francesco
30
Campo San Lorenzo
Borgoloco San Lorenzo
Rio di San Lorenzo
C di Morion
Corta Nova
Scuola Dalmata di San Giorgio degli Schiavoni
2
C del Lion
C d Madonna
C dei Furlani
Fond dei Furlani
Rio di San Severo
16
35
Museo delle Icone
8
15
C d Corona
C d Chiesa
C dei Specchieri
C Fiubera
C d Figher
3
CASTELLO
Campiello dei Greci
Saliz dei Greci
34
C de l'Arco
C del Pestrin
Gondola Service
C d Selvadego
22
Saliz San Provolo
Rio dei Greci
Rio de la Pietà
Campo Bandiera e Moro
14
C dei Albanesi
C delle Rasse
20
Rio del Vin
5
Chiesa di San Zaccaria
Campo San Zaccaria
18
Piazza San Marco
SAN MARCO
23
21
31
Riva degli Schiavoni
San Zaccaria A
Cllo d Pescaria
Riva degli Schiavoni
Rio dei Giardinetti
Giardini Ex Reali
San Zaccaria
San Zaccaria C/D
San Zaccaria B
San Marco Giardinetti
Bacino di San Marco
Canale di San Marco
San Giorgio Maggiore
Campo San Giorgio
Isola di San Giorgio Maggiore

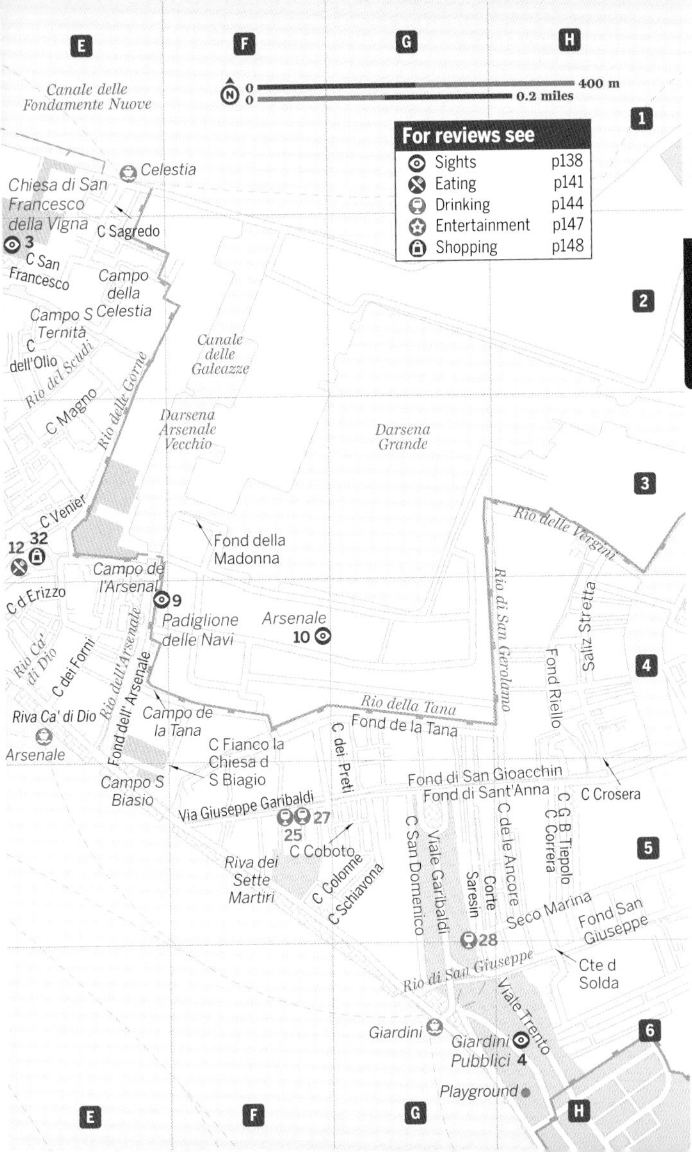
E
F
G
H
0
400 m
0
0.2 miles
N
1
2
3
4
5
6
For reviews see
Sights p138
Eating p141
Drinking p144
Entertainment p147
Shopping p148
Canale delle Fondamente Nuove
Celestia
Chiesa di San Francesco della Vigna
C Sagredo
3
C San Francesco
Campo della Celestia
Campo S Ternità
C dell'Olio
Rio del Scudi
C Magno
Rio delle Gorne
Canale delle Galeazze
Darsena Arsenale Vecchio
Darsena Grande
C Venier
12
32
Fond della Madonna
Campo de l'Arsenal
9
C d Erizzo
Padiglione delle Navi
Arsenale
10
Rio Ca' di Dio
C dei Forni
Rio dell'Arsenale
Fond dell' Arsenale
Riva Ca' di Dio
Arsenale
Campo de la Tana
C Fianco la Chiesa d S Biagio
Campo S Biasio
Rio della Tana
Fond de la Tana
C dei Preti
Rio delle Vergini
Rio di San Gerolamo
Saliz Stretta
Fond Riello
Fond di San Gioacchin
Fond di Sant'Anna
C Crosera
Via Giuseppe Garibaldi
27
25
C Coboto
Riva dei Sette Martiri
C Colonne
C Schiavona
C San Domenico
Viale Garibaldi
Corte Saresin
C de le Ancore
C G B Tiepolo
C Correra
Seco Marina
Fond San Giuseppe
28
Cte d Solda
Rio di San Giuseppe
Viale Trento
Giardini
Giardini Pubblici
4
Playground
E
F
G
H

# Sights

## Zanipolo
BASILICA

1 ◉ MAP P136, B1

Commenced in 1333 but not finished until the 1430s, this vast church is similar in style and scope to the Franciscan Frari in San Polo, which was being raised at the same time. Both oversized structures feature red-brick facades with high-contrast detailing in white stone. After its completion, Zanipolo quickly became the go-to church for ducal funerals and inside you'll find 25 of their lavish tombs, plus works by Bellini, Lorenzetti and Veronese. (Basilica di San Giovanni e Paolo; ☎041 523 59 13; www.basilicasantigiovanniepaolo. it; Campo Zanipolo; adult/reduced €3.50/1.50; ◷9am-6pm Mon-Sat, noon-6pm Sun; ⛴Ospedale)

## Scuola Dalmata di San Giorgio degli Schiavoni
CHURCH

2 ◉ MAP P136, D3

This 15th-century Dalmatian religious-confraternity house is dedicated to favourite Slavic saints George, Tryphon and Jerome, whose lives are captured with precision and glowing early-Renaissance grace by 15th-century master Vittore Carpaccio. (☎041 522 88 28; Calle dei Furlani 3259a; adult/reduced €5/3; ◷1.30-5.30pm Mon, 9.30am-5.30pm Tue-Sat, 9.30am-1.30pm Sun; ⛴San Zaccaria)

## Chiesa di San Francesco della Vigna
CHURCH

3 ◉ MAP P136, E2

Designed and built by Jacopo Sansovino, with a facade by Palladio, this enchanting Franciscan church is one of Venice's most underappreciated attractions. The Madonna positively glows in Bellini's *Madonna and Saints* (1507) in the **Cappella Santa**, just off the flower-carpeted cloister, while swimming angels and strutting birds steal the scene in the delightful *Virgin and Child Enthroned* (c 1455) by Antonio da Negroponte, near the door to the right of the sanctuary. Bring €0.20 to illuminate them. (Campo San Francesco 2786; admission free; ◷8am-12.30pm & 3-7pm; ⛴Celestia)

## Giardini Pubblici
GARDENS

4 ◉ MAP P136, H6

Begun under Napoleon as the city's first public green space, these leafy gardens are now the main home of the Biennale. Around half of the gardens is open to the public all year round; the rest is given over to the permanent **Biennale pavilions**, each representing a different country. Many of them are attractions in their own right, from Carlo Scarpa's daring 1954 raw-concrete-and-glass Venezuelan Pavilion to Denton Corker Marshall's 2015 Australian Pavilion in black granite. (Riva dei Partigiani; ⛴Giardini)

## Chiesa di San Zaccaria

CHURCH

5 MAP P136, C3

When 15th-century Venetian girls showed more interest in sailors than saints, they were sent to the convent adjoining San Zaccaria. The wealth showered on the church by their grateful parents is evident. Masterpieces by Bellini, Titian, Tintoretto and Van Dyck crowd the walls. The star of the show is undoubtedly Giovanni Bellini's *Madonna Enthroned with Child and Saints* (1505), which graces an altar on the left as you enter, and glows like it's plugged into an outlet. (Campo San Zaccaria 4693; admission free; 10am-noon & 4-6pm Mon-Sat, 4-6pm Sun; San Zaccaria)

## Fondazione Querini Stampalia

MUSEUM

6 MAP P136, B2

In 1869 Conte Giovanni Querini Stampalia made a gift of his ancestral 16th-century *palazzo* to the city on the forward-thinking condition that its 700-year-old library operate late-night openings. Savvy drinkers take their *aperitivi* in Carlo Scarpa's modernist garden, while the museum's temporary exhibitions, art-filled salons and rare numismatic collection from the Venetian mint offer an interesting insight into how the Venetian aristocracy collected art. (041 271 14 11; www.querinistampalia.it; Campiello Querini Stampalia 5252; adult/reduced €14/10; 10am-6pm Tue-Sun; San Zaccaria)

## Palazzo Grimani

MUSEUM

7 MAP P136, B2

The Grimani family built their Renaissance *palazzo* (mansion) in 1568 to showcase the extraordinary Graeco-Roman sculpture collection of Cardinal Giovanni Grimani. Now the basis of the Museo Correr (p50) archaeological section, the antiquities were returned to these theatrical, frescoed halls in May 2019 – after a 430-year absence – on a two-year loan. Gathered from Venetian territories all over the Mediterranean, the sculptures demonstrate the epitome of classical beauty that Renaissance humanists so admired. (call centre 041 520 03

*Madonna and Saints* by Bellini

## La Biennale di Venezia

23

The world's most prestigious arts show is something of a misnomer: the Venice Biennale (www.labiennale.org) is actually held every year, but the spotlight alternates between art (odd-numbered years, eg 2017, 2019) and architecture (even-numbered years, eg 2018, 2020). The June–October art biennial presents contemporary art at 30 national pavilions in the Giardini Pubblici, with additional exhibitions in venues across town. The architecture biennial is usually held September to November, filling vast Arsenale boat sheds.

### The History of the Biennale

Venice held its first Biennale in 1895 to reassert its role as global taste-maker and provide an essential corrective to the brutality of the Industrial Revolution. At first the Biennale retained strict control, removing a provocative Picasso from the Spanish Pavilion in 1910, but after WWII, national pavilions asserted their autonomy and the Biennale became an international avant-garde showcase.

### The Pavilions

The Biennale's 29 pavilions tell a fascinating story of 20th-century architecture reflecting national identities from Hungary (futuristic folklore hut) to Canada (ski-lodge cathedral). The most recent addition is the 2015 Australian Pavilion by starchitects Denton Corker Marshall. A black granite box hidden in the foliage, it speaks of the imposition of European settlements on indigenous Australian lands.

### Beyond the Biennale

The city-backed Biennale organisation also runs the Venice International Film Festival each September and organises an International Festival of Contemporary Dance and concert series every summer. For upcoming event listings check the website. To defray substantial costs to the city, there's an entry fee to the main art and architecture shows and film festival premieres – but many ancillary arts programs are free. When the art biennale's in town, book two months ahead for accommodation and a week for restaurants.

45; www.palazzogrimani.org; Ramo Grimani 4858; adult/reduced €5/2, incl Ca' D'Oro €10/4; 10am-7pm Tue-Sun; San Zaccaria)

## Museo delle Icone MUSEUM

8 MAP P136, C3

Glowing colours and all-seeing eyes fill this treasure box of some

80 Byzantine-style icons made in 14th- to 17th-century Italy. Keep your own eye out for the expressive *San Giovanni Climaco*, which shows the saintly author of a Greek spiritual guide distracted from his work by visions of souls diving into hell. (Museum of Icons; ☎041 522 65 81; www.istitutoellenico.org; Campo dei Greci 3412; adult/reduced €4/2; ⏲9am-5pm Sat-Mon; ⛴San Zaccaria)

### Padiglione delle Navi — MUSEUM

9 MAP P136, E4

The Padiglione delle Navi is a vast 2000-sq-metre warehouse containing a fabulous collection of model historic boats, including typical Venetian luggers, gondolas, racing boats, military vessels, a funerary barge and a royal motorboat. (Ships Pavilion; ☎041 24 24; www.visitmuve.it; Fondamenta de la Madonna 2162c; adult/reduced €10/7.50, incl Museo Storico Navale; ⏲11am-6pm summer, to 5pm winter; ⛴Arsenale) It's an annexe of the **Museo Storico Navale** (Naval History Museum; Riva San Biagio 2148; adult/reduced incl Padiglione delle Nave €10/7.50; ⏲10am-6pm summer, to 5pm winter; ⛴Arsenale).

### Arsenale — HISTORIC SITE

10 MAP P136, F4

Founded in 1104, the Arsenale soon became the greatest medieval shipyard in Europe, home to 300 shipping companies employing up to 16,000 people. Capable of turning out a new galley in a day, it is considered a forerunner of mass industrial production. Access is only possible during major events and exhibitions such as Carnival, the Arte Laguna Prize and the art and architecture Biennale, when it forms an awesome backdrop to international exhibitions. (Campo de l'Arsenale; ⛴Arsenale)

### Reali Wellness Spa — SPA

11 MAP P136, A2

In this surprisingly spa-starved city, the Hotel ai Reali's wellness centre offers a sanctuary of Asian-inspired wellness. Instead of being banished to the basement, as is usually the case, the Reali's spa is on the top floor where light floods into the Turkish bath and soothes you in your 'emotional' shower. A range of Thai massages and beauty treatments is offered. (☎041 241 59 16; www.hotelaireali.com; Campo de la Fava 5527; 4hr sessions €25; ⏲10am-9pm; ⛴Rialto)

## Eating

### Trattoria Corte Sconta — VENETIAN €€€

12 MAP P136, E3

Well-informed visitors and celebrating locals seek out this vine-covered *corte sconta* (hidden courtyard) for its trademark seafood antipasti and imaginative house-made pasta. Inventive flavour pairings transform the classics: clams zing with ginger;

prawn and courgette linguine is recast with an earthy dash of saffron; and the roast eel loops like the Brenta river in a drizzle of balsamic reduction. (041 522 70 24; www.cortescontavenezia.it; Calle del Pestrin 3886; meals €45-55; 12.30-2pm & 7-9.30pm Tue-Sat, closed Jan & Aug; ; Arsenale)

## Alle Testiere

VENETIAN **€€€**

13 MAP P136, B2

Make a reservation for one of the two evening sittings at this tiny restaurant and come prepared for Bruno Gavagnin's beautifully plated seafood feasts. Subtle spices such as ginger, cinnamon and orange zest recall Venice's trading past with the East. (041 522 72 20; www.osterialletestiere.it; Calle del Mondo Novo 5801; meals €45-60; 12.30-3pm & 7-11pm Tue-Sat; Rialto)

## CoVino

VENETIAN **€€**

14 MAP P136, D3

Tiny CoVino has only 14 seats but demonstrates bags of ambition with its inventive, seasonal menu inspired by the Venetian terroir. Speciality products are selected from Slow Food Foundation producers, and the charming waiters make enthusiastic recommendations from the wine list. Only a three-course set menu is available at dinner; however, you can choose from two fixed-price options at lunch. (041 241 27 05; www.covinovenezia.com; Calle del Pestrin 3829;

One of the Biennale pavilions in the Giardini Pubblici (p138)

fixed-price menu lunch €27-38, dinner €40; 12.45-2.30pm & 7pm-midnight Thu-Mon; ; Arsenale)

### Local

VENETIAN €€€

15 MAP P136, D3

Although he's cooked in fine-dining establishments such as Noma, chef Matteo Tagliapietra grew up on the fishing island of Burano. As such, his simple, seasonal cooking is rooted in the lagoon and his dishes, while creative, remain honest and flavourful. Highlights of the ever-changing menu include gnocchi with mallard, mackerel with red cabbage, and the chocolate *barene* (sandbank) dessert. (041 241 11 28; www.ristorantelocal.com; Salizada dei Greci 3303; meals €75; noon-2pm & 7-10pm Thu-Mon, 7-10pm Wed; ; San Zaccaria)

### Al Giardinetto da Severino

VENETIAN €€

16 MAP P136, C3

Date nights don't come better than sitting among a sea of greenery in Al Giardinetto's vine-covered courtyard. For nearly 70 years the Bastianello-Parmesan family have run this restaurant in the former chapel of the 15th-century Palazzo Zorzi. In that time they've perfected traditional dishes such as crab pasta, bean soup and veal schnitzel. (041 528 53 32; www.algiardinetto.it; Salizada Zorzi 4928; meals €35-45; noon-3pm & 7-10pm Fri-Wed Feb-Dec; San Zaccaria)

### Lovers' Alley

Under the arch of the covered passageway **Sotoportego dei Preti** (Arsenale) is hidden a reddish, heart-shaped stone about the size of a hand. Local lore has it that couples that touch it together will remain in love forever. Not ready to commit just yet? This is also a nice private spot for a smooch

### Didovich

DELI €

17 MAP P136, A2

With outside seating on pretty Campo Santa Marina, cheerful Didovich offers the rare opportunity to sit down for a cooked breakfast. Otherwise you join the locals propping up the counter, sipping coffee and munching on croissants and *fritelle* (doughnuts). At lunchtime, sweets change to savouries and takeaway homemade pasta or *polpette* (meatballs). (041 523 00 17; Campo Santa Marina 5908; pastries €1.10, mains €8-10; 7am-7.30pm Mon-Sat; Rialto)

### Wildner

VENETIAN €€€

18 MAP P136, C4

Occupying a glass pavilion on the Riva, Pensione Wildner's long-standing restaurant serves delicious takes on traditional Venetian dishes, such as octopus on lentils and veal liver on polenta. The prime waterfront position makes it a perfect place for lunch. The gourmet sandwiches and wine pairings are great value, as is the lunch special menu (two courses and wine for €20). (041 522 74 63; www.hotelwildner.com; Riva degli Schiavoni 4161; sandwich & wine pairings €20-30, meals €44-55; noon-10pm Wed-Mon; San Zaccaria)

### Osteria Ruga di Jaffa
OSTERIA €€

19 MAP P136, B2

Set on busy Ruga Giuffa, this *osteria* has artsy Murano lamps and seafaring paraphernalia. You should be able to spot it by the gondoliers packing out the tables at lunchtime; they come to feast on lagoon crustaceans, homemade pasta and hearty plates of oven-roasted pork. Plates of *cicheti* (Venetian tapas) can also be taken at the bar with a *spritz*. (041 241 10 62; www.osteriarugadijaffa.it; Ruga Giuffa 4864; meals €15-30; 10am-11.30pm; San Zaccaria)

### Trattoria alla Rivetta
VENETIAN €€

20 MAP P136, B3

Tucked behind the Ponte San Provolo, this trattoria hums with the chatter of contented diners even in the dead of winter. It is staffed by a clutch of senior waiters in jovial red waistcoats, who'll cordially serve you platters of lagoon fare such as raw seafood antipasti, pasta with clams and *fritto misto* (mixed fried seafood). (041 528 73 02; Salizada San Provolo 4625; meals €25-40; 10.30am-10.30pm Tue-Sun; San Zaccaria) .

## Drinking

### Bar Dandolo
COCKTAIL BAR

21 MAP P136, B4

Dress to the nines and swan straight past the 'hotel guests only' sign to the glamorous bar that fills the grand hall of the 14th-century Palazzo Dandolo. Murano chandeliers reflect off gilt edges and silk furnishings, while snappily dressed staff effortlessly descend with signature Vesper martinis and bottomless bowls of snacks. (041 522 64 80; www.danielihotelvenice.com; Riva degli Schiavoni 4196; 9.30am-1am; San Zaccaria)

### Bacaro Risorto
BAR

22 MAP P136, C3

Just a footbridge away from San Marco, this shoebox of a corner bar offers quality wines and abundant *cicheti* (Venetian tapas), including *crostini* (open-faced sandwiches) heaped with *sarde in saor* (sardines in a sweet and sour sauce), soft cheeses and melon tightly swaddled in prosciutto. Note that opening times are 'flexible'. (Campo San Provolo 4700; 8am-1am; San Zaccaria)

### Bar Terrazza Danieli
BAR

23 MAP P136, B4

Gondolas glide in to dock along the quay, while across the lagoon the white-marble edifice of Palladio's San Giorgio Maggiore turns from gold to pink in the waters of the canal: this is the late-afternoon scene from the Hotel Danieli's top-floor balcony bar and it definitely calls for a toast. Linger over a *spritz* (cocktail made with prosecco) or cocktail. (041 522 64 80; www.danielihotelvenice.com; Riva degli Schiavoni 4196; 3-7pm May-Sep; San Zaccaria)

## Enoiteca Mascareta VENETO €€

24 MAP P136, B2

Once more of a wine bar than a restaurant, Mascareta is now very much an eatery, serving champagne and oysters or more rustic fare such as guinea fowl. With more than 1000 labels of wine available to try by the glass, however, Enoiteca Mascareta has not betrayed its roots as a top-class vintner. (041 523 07 44; www.ostemaurolorenzon.com; Calle Lunga Santa Maria Formosa 5183; meals €35-45; 7pm-2am; Rialto)

## Strani BAR

25 MAP P136, F5

There's always a party on at Strani thanks to its excellent selection of beers on tap, well-priced glasses of Veneto wines and platters of *sopressa* (soft salami). A plethora of *cicheti* (Venetian tapas) keeps drinkers fuelled for late-night jam sessions with the locals. (041 099 14 34; Via Garibaldi 1582; 7.30am-1am summer, noon-10pm winter; Giardini)



Fresh oysters

### Venice Music Gourmet

Hosted in historic palaces, these gourmet musical evenings promise stirring tunes from Vivaldi and Bach, as well as Italian jazz legends, accompanied by a multicourse dinner of lagoon delights. It's exactly how Venetians past would have heard the latest tracks amid a convivial group of guests knocking back first-class glasses of Franciacorta and forkfuls of sarde in saor (grilled sardines in a sweet and sour sauce).

### Osteria Al Portego

BAR

26 MAP P136, A2

This walk-in closet somehow manages to distribute wine, craft beer and *cicheti* to the overflowing crowd of young Venetians in approximate order of arrival. Wine is cheap and plentiful, and the bar groans with classic nibbles. If that's not enough, make a dash for one of the five tables around the back where enormous plates of seafood are served. (041 522 90 38; www.osteriaalportego.org; Calle de la Malvasia 6014; 10.30am-2.30pm & 5.30-10.30pm; Rialto)

### El Rèfolo

BAR

27 MAP P136, F5

Although the bars along Via Garibaldi may look interchangeable, the queue for El Rèfolo's pavement tables says otherwise. Part of the draw is the ever-friendly Massimiliano dispensing Italian microbrews and glasses of wine, as well as the plump sandwiches and summertime live music. (www.elrefolo.it; Via Garibaldi 1580; 11.30am-12.30am Tue-Sun; Giardini)

### Serra dei Giardini

CAFE

28 MAP P136, G5

This attractive iron-framed greenhouse was built in 1894 to house the palms used in Biennale events. It rapidly expanded into a social hub and a centre for propagation: many plants grown here adorned the municipal flowerbeds of the Lido and the ballrooms of aristocratic *palazzi* (mansions). Restored in 2010, it now houses a cafe and hosts events, exhibitions and workshops. (041 296 03 60; www.serradeigiardini.org; Viale Garibaldi 1254; admission free; 10am-8pm; Giardini)

### Rosa Salva

CAFE

29 MAP P136, B1

For over a century, Rosa Salva has been serving tea, pastries and ice creams to the passing trade on Campo Zanipolo. Inside the 1930s throwback interior, ladies take *tramezzini* (triangular, stacked sandwiches) and trays of *tè con limone* (tea with lemon) at marble-topped tables while, outside, sun-seekers sip *spritz* (cocktail made with prosecco) and children slurp ice creams. (☎041 522 79 49; www.rosasalva.it; Campo Zanipolo 6779; 8am-8pm; Ospedale)

# Entertainment

## Laboratorio Occupato Morion

LIVE MUSIC

30 MAP P136, D2

When not busy staging environmental protests or avant-garde performance art, this counterculture social centre throws one hell of a party, with performances by bands from around the Veneto. Events are announced via posters thrown up around town and on its Facebook page. (www.facebook.com/laboratorioccupatomorion; Salizada San Francesco 2951; Celestia)

## Collegium Ducale

CLASSICAL MUSIC

31 MAP P136, B4

Spend a perfectly enjoyable evening in prison with this six-member chamber orchestra, which performs Vivaldi's *Four Seasons* in the grand hall rather than the cells. On alternate nights opera singers tackle everything from Mozart to Gershwin accompanied only by a piano. (☎041 98 42 52; www.collegiumducale.com; Palazzo delle Prigioni 4209; adult/reduced €27.50/22; San Zaccaria)

Ponte della Paglia and Palazzo Ducal (p40)

### Vivaldi's Orphan Orchestra

Over the centuries, Venetian musicians developed a reputation for playing music as though their lives depended on it – which at times wasn't far from the truth. With shrinking 17th-century trade revenues, the state took the quixotic step of underwriting musical education for orphan girls, and the investment yielded surprising returns.

Among the maestri hired to conduct orphan-girl orchestras was Antonio Vivaldi (1678–1741), whose 30-year tenure yielded hundreds of concertos and popularised Venetian baroque music across Europe. Visitors spread word of extraordinary performances by orphan girls, and the city became a magnet for novelty-seeking, moneyed socialites.

Modern visitors to Venice can still see music and opera performed in the same venues as in Vivaldi's day – including Tiepolo-frescoed **La Pietà** (041 522 21 71; www.pietavenezia.org; Riva degli Schiavoni; €3; 10am-6pm Tue-Sun; San Zaccaria), the *ospedaletto* (orphanage) where Vivaldi was the musical director.

# Shopping

## Atelier Alessandro Merlin

HOMEWARES

32 MAP P136, E3

Enjoy your breakfast in the nude, on a horse or atop a jellyfish – Alessandro Merlin paints them all on striking black and white cappuccino cups and saucers. Homoerotic-art lovers will recognise the influence of Tom of Finland in the ultra-masculine, well-endowed nude dudes, but the sgraffito technique Alessandro uses on some of his work dates back to Roman times. (041 522 58 95; Calle del Pestrin 3876; 10am-noon & 3-7pm Mon, Tue & Sat, 3-7pm Fri & Sun; Arsenale)

## Kalimala

SHOES

33 MAP P136, A2

Sleek belts with brushed-steel buckles, satchels, manbags and knee-high red boots: Kalimala makes beautiful leather goods in practical, modern styles. Shoes, sandals and gloves are crafted from vegetable-cured cowhide and dyed in a mix of earthy tones and vibrant lapis blues. Given the natural tanning and top-flight leather, prices are remarkably reasonable, with handmade shoes starting at €135. (041 528 35 96; www.kalimalavenezia.it; Salizada San Lio 5387; 9.30am-7.30pm Mon-Sat; Rialto)

## Bragorà
FASHION & ACCESSORIES

34 MAP P136, D3

Bragorà is a multipurpose space: part shop, service centre and cultural hub. Its upcycled products include beach bags sewn out of boat sails, toy gondolas fashioned from drink cans, belts made from bike tyres and jewellery crafted from springs. There's an excellent range of witty tees on Venetian themes and you can even print your own. (041 319 08 64; www.bragora.it; Salizada Sant'Antonin 3496; 9.30am-7.30pm Mon-Sat, 10.30am-6.30pm Sun; Arsenale)

## Paolo Brandolisio
ARTS & CRAFTS

35 MAP P136, C3

Beneath all the marble and gilt, Venice is a city of wood, long supported by its carpenters, caulkers, oar-makers and gilders. Master woodcarver Paolo Brandolisio continues the traditions, crafting the sinuous *forcola* (rowlock) that supports the gondolier's oar. Made of walnut or cherry wood, each is crafted specifically for boat and gondolier. Miniature replicas are on sale. (041 522 41 55; Sotoportego Corte Rota 4725; 9am-1pm & 3-7pm Mon-Fri; San Zaccaria)

## Ballarin
ANTIQUES

36 MAP P136, C2

If you're looking for something distinctively Venetian, check out this Aladdin's cave. An old-fashioned dealer and artisan restorer, Valter Ballarin has a knack for tracking down period furnishings, hand-painted glassware, prints, books, toys and lamps. The best souvenir is a handful of colourful, hand-blown glass flowers from dismembered Murano chandeliers. (347 7792492; Calle del Cafetier 6482; 10am-1pm & 4-6.30pm Mon-Sat; Ospedale)

## Artigianato Veneziano
JEWELLERY

37 MAP P136, B2

Utilising traditional Murano techniques and materials, including oxides and resins, Sabina Melinato conjures up contemporary glass and costume jewellery. Her deco-inspired glass pendants are so highly polished they look like lacquerwork – just what you'd expect from a teacher at Murano's International School of Glass. (041 523 57 34; Calle Lunga Santa Maria Formosa 5184; 9.30am-12.30pm & 3.30-7.30pm Mon-Sat; Ospedale)

## Qshop
BOOKS

In addition to its sumptuous range of art and design books, the shop of the **Fondazione Querini Stampalia** (6 MAP P136, B2) offers a highly curated selection of glass, jewellery, household items, silverware and textiles. Pieces from design greats such as Carlo Scarpa, Carlo Moretti and San Lorenzo sit beside the work of emerging talents. (041 523 44 11; www.querinistampalia.it; Campiello Querini Stampalia 5252; 10am-6pm Tue-Sun; San Zaccaria)

Explore

# The Lagoon & the Islands

*Other cities have suburban sprawl and malls; Venice has a teal-blue lagoon dotted with photogenic islands and rare wildlife. Outlying islands range from celebrated glass centres and former Byzantine capitals to beach resorts and arty isles.*

## The Short List

- ***Basilica di San Giorgio Maggiore (p152)*** *Immersing yourself in the serenity of Palladio's eye-catching church and ascending its bell tower for spectacular San Marco views.*
- ***Basilica di Santa Maria Assunta (p154)*** *Engaging with angelic visions and demonic depictions at the lagoon's oldest church on Torcello.*
- ***Basilica dei SS Maria e Donato (p157)*** *Checking out golden mosaics and a spectacular marbled floor at Murano's medieval church.*
- ***Fondazione Giorgio Cini (p163)*** *Taking in Palladio's cloister, Longhena's library, and an elaborate garden maze on the Isola di San Giorgio Maggiore.*

## Getting There & Around

**Vaporetto** Giudecca: lines 2, 4.1, 4.2 and N (night) from San Marco or Dorsoduro; San Giorgio Maggiore: line 2 from San Zaccaria; Lido: lines 1, 2, 5.1, 5.2, 6, 8, 10 and 14; Murano: lines 3, 4.1 or 4.2, lines 12 and 13 stop only at Faro; Burano, Mazzorbo and Torcello: line 12 from Fondamente Nove or Murano-Faro stop; line 9 from Burano also heads to Torcello; Le Vignole and Sant'Erasmo: line 13 from Fondamente Nove via Murano-Faro.

The Lagoon & the Islands Map on p162

**Murano Island (p156)** JAYSI/SHUTTERSTOCK ©

Top Experience

# Admire the view from Basilica di San Giorgio Maggiore

*Designed by Andrea Palladio for maximum dazzle, this Benedictine abbey church was built between 1565 and 1610 and positioned on its own island facing San Marco. Palladio chose white Istrian stone to stand out against the blue lagoon waters, and set it at an angle to create visual drama while also ensuring that it catches the sun all afternoon.*

MAP P162, D3

041 522 78 27

www.abbaziasangiorgio.it

Isola di San Giorgio Maggiore

bell tower adult/reduced €6/4

9am-6pm

San Giorgio Maggiore

## Palladio's Facade

Palladio's radical facade gracefully solved the problem bedevilling Renaissance church design: how to graft a triangular, classical pediment onto a Christian church with a high, central nave and lower side aisles. Palladio's solution: use one pediment to crown the nave, and a lower, half-pediment to span each side aisle. The two interlock with rhythmic harmony, while prominent three-quarter columns, deeply incised capitals and sculptural niches create depth with clever shadow-play. Above the facade rises a brick *campanile* (bell tower) with a conical copper spire and a cap of Istrian stone.

## Interior

Likewise, the interior is an uncanny combination of brightness and serenity. Sunlight enters through high thermal windows and is then diffused by acres of white stucco. Floors inlaid with white, red and black stone draw the eye toward the altar. With its rigorous application of classical motifs, it's reminiscent of a Roman theatre.

## Tintorettos

Two outstanding late works by Tintoretto flank the church's altar. On one side hangs his *Collection of Manna;* on the other side, *Last Supper* depicts Christ and his apostles in a scene that looks suspiciously like a 16th-century Venetian tavern, with a cat and dog angling for scraps. Nearby hangs what is considered to be Tintoretto's final masterpiece, the moving *Deposition of Christ.*

### ★ Top Tips

- Take the lift to the top of the bell tower, where you can catch a unique view back across the lagoon – it's cheaper than San Marco's *campanile* and you won't have to queue.
- Tintoretto's final work, the moving *Deposition of Christ* (1594), hangs within the Cappella delle Deposizione, which is accessed from the sanctuary but is only open for Mass.

### Take a Break

There's nowhere to eat on the island itself so jump on the number 2 *vaporetto* to Giudecca for a quick bite at La Palanca (p166).

For a more upmarket meal, try Trattoria ai Cacciatori (p168).

Top Experience

# Experience the ages at Basilica di Santa Maria Assunta & Torcello

*Life choices are presented in no uncertain terms in Santa Maria Assunta's vivid cautionary tale: look ahead to a golden afterlife amid saints and a beatific Madonna, or turn your back on her to face the wrath of a devil gloating over lost souls. In existence since the 7th century, this former cathedral is the lagoon's oldest Byzantine-Romanesque structure.*

MAP P162, F1

041 73 01 19

Piazza Torcello, Torcello

adult/reduced €5/4, incl museum & campanile €12/10

10.30am-5.30pm

Torcello

### Madonna & Last Judgment Mosaics

The restrained brick exterior betrays no hint of the colourful scene that unfolds as you enter. The Madonna rises in the east like the sun above a field of Torcello poppies in the 12th-century **apse mosaic** (pictured), while the back wall vividly depicts the dire consequences of dodging biblical commandments. This extraordinary **Last Judgment mosaic** shows the Adriatic as a sea nymph ushering souls lost at sea towards St Peter, while a sneaky devil tips the scales of justice and the Antichrist's minions drag sinners into hell.

### Chapel Mosaics & Other Key Works

The right-hand chapel is capped with another 12th-century mosaic showing Christ flanked by angels and Sts Augustine, Ambrose, Martin and Gregory amid symbolic plants: lilies (representing purity), wheat and grapes (representing the bread and wine of the Eucharist), and poppies (evoking Torcello's island setting).

The polychrome marble floor is another medieval masterpiece, with swirling designs and interlocking wheels symbolising eternal life. Saints line up atop the gilded **iconostasis**, their gravity foiled by a Byzantine screen teeming with peacocks, rabbits and other fanciful beasts.

### Museo di Torcello

Relics of Torcello's 7th- to 11th-century Byzantine empire are shown inside 13th-century Palazzo del Consiglio, home to the **Museo di Torcello** (041 73 07 61; www.museoditorcello.provincia.venezia.it; Piazza Torcello, Torcello; adult/reduced €3/1.50, incl basilica €8/6; 10.30am-5.30pm Tue-Sun; Torcello). Exquisite mosaic fragments here show glass mastery achieved in Torcello before Murano entered the business, while upstairs archives contain Graeco-Roman artefacts from the lost civilisation of Altinum.

### ★ Top Tips

- Climb the *campanile* (€5) at the rear for the heavenly view over the swampy islands, which gives a fascinating insight into what Venice itself must once have looked like.
- An audio guide (€2) gives further details of the church and its artworks.
- Various combo tickets are offered including the church, *campanile*, audio guide and the neighbouring museum (which is closed on Mondays).

### Take a Break

Locanda Cipriani (p165) offers bellinis and duck pasta in a splendid rose garden. Otherwise, hop the *vaporetto* to Mazzorbo for lagoon-inspired fare in the vineyard of Venissa Osteria (p166).

Walking Tour

# Murano Art Glass

*Unrivalled masters of art glass since the 10th century, Venice's glass artisans moved to Murano in the 13th century to contain fornace (furnace) fire hazards. Trade secrets were so jealously guarded that glass masters who left the city were threatened with assassination. Today, Murano glass masters ply their trade along Fondamenta dei Vetrai and Ramo di Mula, and their wares are unmatched.*

**Start** Basilica dei SS Maria e Donato; vaporetto Museo

**Finish** Marina e Susanna Sent Studio; vaporetto Colonna

**Length** 1.5km; ¾ hour

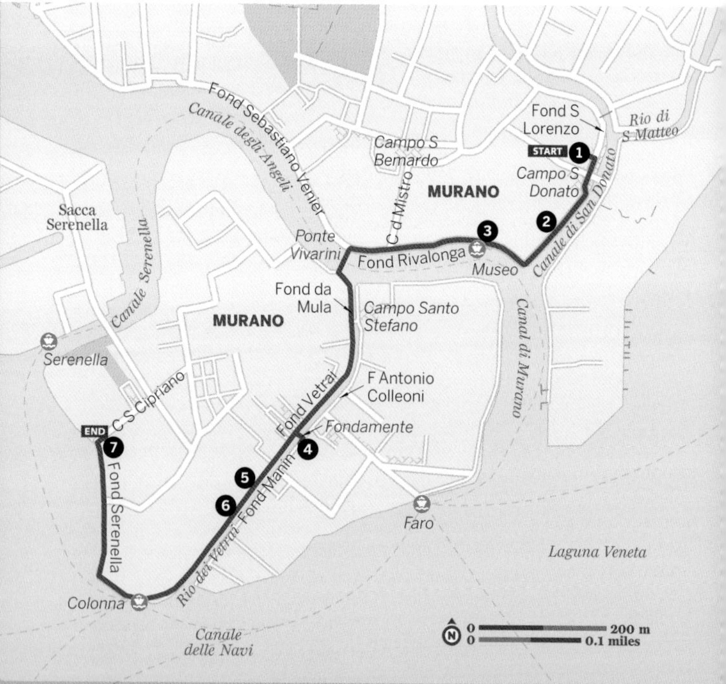

## ❶ Basilica Bones & Mosaics

In medieval **Basilica dei SS Maria e Donato** (www.sandonatomurano.it; Campo San Donato, Murano; admission free; ⏰9am-6pm Mon-Sat, 12.30-6pm Sun; ⛴Museo) a 12th-century gilded-glass mosaic Madonna created in Murano's *fornaci* graces the apse and the bones of a dragon hang behind the altar – according to legend the dragon was slayed by St Donatus of Arezzo, whose remains also rest here.

## ❷ Glass Museum

Since 1861, Murano's glass-making prowess has been celebrated at the **Museo del Vetro** (Glass Museum; ☎041 243 49 14; www.museovetro.visitmuve.it; Fondamenta Giustinian 8, Murano; adult/reduced €14/11.50, free with Museum Pass; ⏰10am-5pm; ⛴Museo) in Palazzo Giustinian and renovations finally do justice to the fabulous collection. Upstairs eight rooms have beautifully curated displays of objects dating back to the 5th century BC.

## ❸ Davide Penso Beadwork

**Davide Penso** (☎041 73 98 19; www.davidepenso.com; Fondamenta Riva Longa 48, Murano; ⏰10am-6pm Mon-Sat; ⛴Museo) has taken the art of bead-making global, with African-inspired necklaces exhibited at Boston's Fine Arts Museum. Lampworked beads in essential shapes are strung onto modern necklaces and bracelets that look ancient.

## ❹ Cutting-Edge at ElleElle

Nason Moretti has made modernist magic in glass since the 1950s, and at **ElleElle** (☎041 527 48 66; www.elleellemurano.com; Fondamenta Manin 52, Murano; ⏰10.30am-6pm; ⛴Faro) is breaking new ground with collections for New York's MoMA. Prices start at €30 for blown-glass drinking glasses.

## ❺ Modern Classics at Venini

Of the big houses, **Venini** (☎041 273 72 04; www.venini.it; Fondamenta dei Vetrai 47, Murano; ⏰9.30am-6pm Mon-Sat; ⛴Colonna) remains the most relevant, defining modernist trends since the 1930s. Collaborations feature design greats like Carlo Scarpa and Fabio Novembre, who created giant glass 'Happy Pills' for Venini.

## ❻ Winged Goblets at Toffolo

Classic gold-leafed winged goblets and mind-boggling miniatures are the legendary master glass-blower's trademarks at **Cesare Toffolo** (☎041 73 64 60; www.toffolo.com; Fondamenta dei Vetrai 37, Murano; ⏰10am-6pm; ⛴Colonna), but you'll also find some dramatic departures such as jet-black vases.

## ❼ Sent Studio Jewels

The Sent sisters are fourth-generation glassmakers, and their new light-filled, exposed-concrete **Marina e Susanna Sent Studio** (☎041 527 46 65 www.marinaesusannasent.com; Fondamenta Serenella 20; ⏰10am-5pm Mon-Fri) is as strikingly modern as their jewellery.

Walking Tour

# Getting Creative in Giudecca

*Once the glamorous garden-villa island getaway of Venice's elite, Giudecca became a military-industrial complex in the 19th century. Now its brutalist factories, barracks and arsenals are being creatively repurposed into industrial-cool hubs by Venice's creative class. Whether your creative aspirations are in design, art, cuisine, theatre, architecture, music or photography, Giudecca is an island of inspiration.*

**Start** Fortuny Tessuti Artistici; vaporetto Palanca

**Finish** Casa dei Tre Oci; vaporetto Zitelle

**Length** 2km; one hour

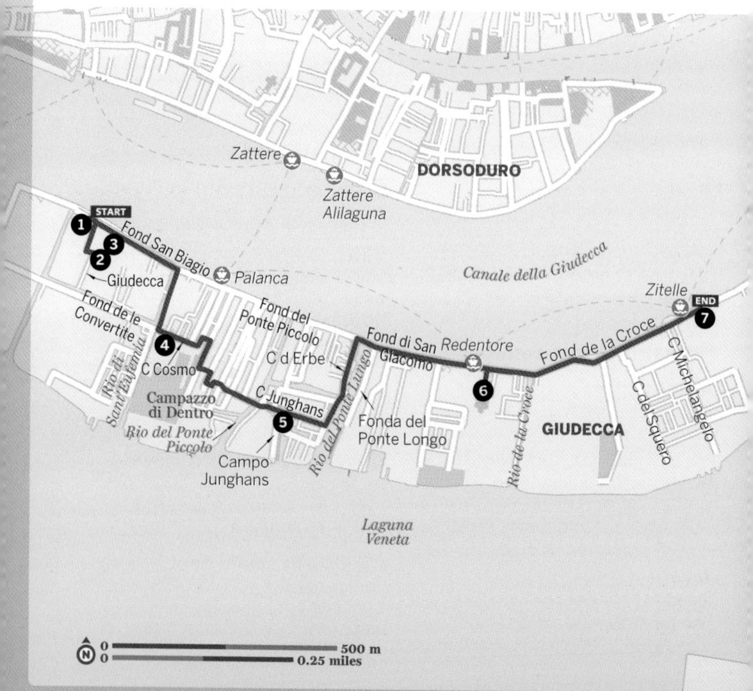

## ❶ Design Schemes at Fortuny

Find out why Marcel Proust waxed rhapsodic over Fortuny's silken cottons printed with art nouveau patterns at **Fortuny Tessuti Artistici** (393 8257651; www.fortuny.com; Fondamenta San Biagio 805, Giudecca; 10am-6pm Mon-Fri; Palanca). Fabrication methods have been jealously guarded in the garden studio for a century.

## ❷ Brewery Events Space

Non-profit gallery **Spazio Punch** (www.spaziopunch.com) has transformed Giudecca's derelict beer factory into an occasional venue for temporary art, design and fashion events, which take place several times a year.

## ❸ Emerging Art at Giudecca 795

Kickstart art collections with original works by emerging local artists at **Giudecca 795** (340 8798327; www.giudecca795.com; Fondamenta San Biagio 795, Giudecca; admission free; 6-8pm Tue-Fri & Sun, 4-8pm Sat; Palanca) – before they get discovered at the Venice Biennale.

## ❹ Holy Artisans!

The cloister of the former Convent of Sts Cosmas and Damian has been re-purposed as **Artigiani del Chiostro** (Campo San Cosma 620a, Giudecca; hr vary; Palanca), a base for independent artisans to ply their craft. You'll find traditional mask makers, antique restorers, artists, metal workers, glass-blowers and many, many cats.

## ❺ Arsenal Theatrics

Make art, not war at this modern theatre built on the site of a former arsenal. **Teatro Junghans** (041 241 19 74; www.accademiateatraleveneta.com; Campo Junghans 494b, Giudecca; prices vary; ; Redentore) stages original works and offers workshops on costume design and *commedia dell'arte* (traditional masked theatre) .

## ❻ Triumph at Il Rendentore

Palladio's 1577–92 **Il Redentore** (Church of the Most Holy Redeemer; www.chorusvenezia.org; Campo del SS Redentore 194, Giudecca; adult/reduced €3/1.50, with Chorus Pass free; 10.30am-4.30pm Mon-Sat; Redentore) is a triumph of white marble celebrating the city's deliverance from the Black Death. Paolo Piazza's strikingly modern 1619 *Gratitude of Venice for Liberation* shows the city held aloft by angels in sobering shades of grey.

## ❼ Photography at Tre Oci

The view of San Marco from the three porthole windows at **Casa dei Tre Oci** (041 241 23 32; www.treoci.org; Fondamenta de le Zitelle 43, Giudecca; adult/reduced €12/10; 10am-7pm Wed-Mon; Zitelle) may inspire your own photographic masterpieces, as may the shows of contemporary photography and art held here..

Walking Tour

# Beaches & Bars on the Lido

*Beach chairs and bronzed lifeguards may seem a world apart from muggy, ripe central Venice in summer, but they're only a 15-minute ferry ride away. Sandy beaches line the seaward side of the Lido; they're packed in summer although their gentle gradient makes them perfect for toddlers but a little frustrating for adults. For adults, there's refreshing cocktails and epic summer-weekend DJ sessions and beach concerts.*

**Start** Lido on Bike; vaporetto Lido SME

**Finish** Pachuka; bus A

**Length** 3km; 1½ hours

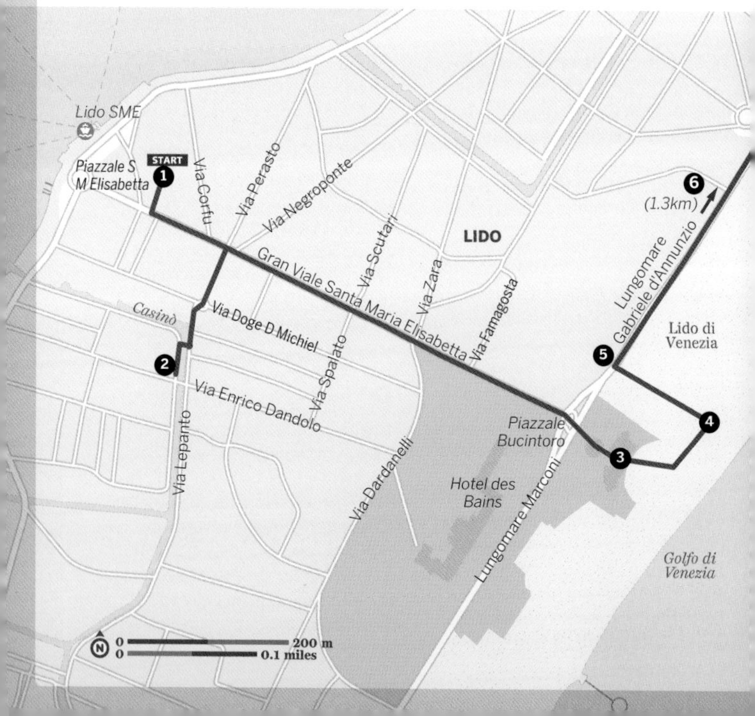

## ❶ Beach-Hop by Bicycle

To tour at your own pace, rent a set of wheels from friendly **Lido on Bike** (041 526 80 19; www.lidoonbike.it; Gran Viale Santa Maria Elisabetta 21b, Lido; bicycle rental per 90min/day €5/10; 9am-7pm summer; Lido SME). Reasonable prices include a free map with recommended routes. Identification showing you're at least 18 is required.

## ❷ Drink Like a Fish at al Mercà

Located in the old Lido fish market, **al Mercà** (041 243 16 63; www.osteriaalmerca.it; Via Enrico Dandolo 17a, Lido; meals €30-43, 3-course meat/fish menu €15/20; noon-2.30pm & 6.45-9.30pm daily summer, noon-2.30pm & 6.45-9.30pm Thu-Sat & noon-2.30pm Sun winter; Lido SME) is a year-round draw for its abundant *cicheti* (Venetian tapas), outdoor seating and well-priced wine by the glass. Take a pew at one of the marble counters and order up a seafood storm of *folpetti* (mini octopus), fried *schìe* (shrimp) and creamy salt cod.

## ❸ Summer Events at Blue Moon

From afar, the domed semicircular structure of **Blue Moon** (www.veneziaspiagge.it; Piazzale Bucintoro 1, Lido; admission free; 10am-6.30pm summer; ; Lido SME) looks like an alien landing. A series of ramps and staircases lead to a bar, a restaurant, a raised dance floor and a viewing platform. In su the hive-like structure hums daytime events and activitie



## ❹ Hit the Public Beach

This is the closest *spiaggia comunale* (public beach) to the ferry and on sunny weekends it can get packed. Spread out your towel on the sand with impunity; most other beaches on the island are commercialised, with rows of changing sheds and deck chairs for hire.

## ❺ Happy Hour on El Pecador

No you're not suffering from heatstroke: that really is a red, double-decker bus parked along the Lungomare, attracting an alternative crowd to impromptu beach parties. Head to **El Pecador** (324 8373715; Lungomare Gabriele d'Annunzio, Lido; sandwiches €3-6; 10am-2am Apr-Sep; Lido SME) for some of the Lido's finest stuffed sandwiches and *spritz* (prosecco cocktails), and claim a seat on the canopied top deck.

## ❻ Party at Pachuka

The most reliable of the Lido's summertime dance spots, **Pachuka** (041 770 147; www.pachuka.com; Viale Umberto Klinger, Lido; hr vary; A) works year-round as a snack bar and pizzeria but on summer weekend nights it cranks up as a beachside dance club, too. Expect live music and DJ sets right on the beach.

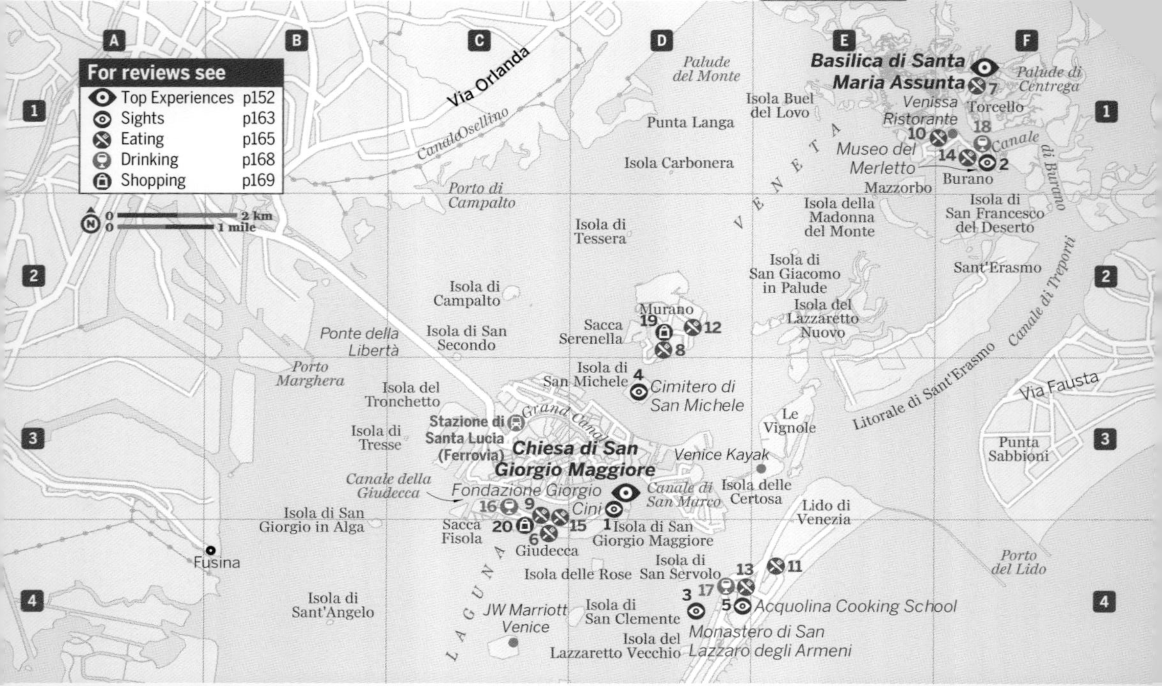
For reviews see
Top Experiences p152
Sights p163
Eating p165
Drinking p168
Shopping p169
0 2 km
0 1 mile
Via Orlanda
Canale Osellino
Porto di Campalto
Palude del Monte
Punta Langa
Isola Carbonera
Isola Buel del Lovo
Basilica di Santa Maria Assunta
Venissa Ristorante
Torcello
Palude di Centrega
Canale di Burano
Museo del Merletto
Burano
Mazzorbo
Isola della Madonna del Monte
Isola di San Francesco del Deserto
Isola di Tessera
Sant'Erasmo
Isola di San Giacomo in Palude
Isola del Lazzaretto Nuovo
Canale di Treporti
Isola di Campalto
Murano
Sacca Serenella
Ponte della Libertà
Isola di San Secondo
Porto Marghera
Isola del Tronchetto
Isola di San Michele
Cimitero di San Michele
Litorale di Sant'Erasmo
Via Fausta
Le Vignole
Punta Sabbioni
Grand Canal
Stazione di Santa Lucia (Ferrovia)
Isola di Tresse
Chiesa di San Giorgio Maggiore
Venice Kayak
Canale della Giudecca
Fondazione Giorgio Cini
Canale di San Marco
Isola delle Certosa
Lido di Venezia
Isola di San Giorgio in Alga
Sacca Fisola
Isola di San Giorgio Maggiore
Giudecca
Fusina
Porto del Lido
Isola delle Rose
Isola di San Servolo
Acquolina Cooking School
Isola di Sant'Angelo
LAGUNA VENETA
JW Marriott Venice
Isola di San Clemente
Isola del Lazzaretto Vecchio
Monastero di San Lazzaro degli Armeni

# Sights

## Fondazione Giorgio Cini CULTURAL CENTRE

1 MAP P162, D3

In 1951, industrialist and art patron Vittorio Cini – a survivor of Dachau – acquired the monastery of San Giorgio and restored it in memory of his son, Giorgio Cini. The rehabilitated complex is an architectural treasure incorporating designs by Andrea Palladio and Baldassare Longhena. Tours allow you to stroll through the cloisters, visit the refectory and libraries, and gaze down on the Borges Labyrinth – an intricate garden maze built to honour Argentinian writer Jorge Luis Borges. (041 271 02 37; www.cini.it; Isola di San Giorgio Maggiore; adult/reduced €13/10; tours 10am-6pm daily Apr-Nov, to 4pm Wed-Mon Dec-Mar; San Giorgio Maggiore)

## Museo del Merletto MUSEUM

2 MAP P162, F1

Burano's Lace Museum tells the story of a craft that cut across social boundaries, endured for centuries and evoked the epitome of sophistication reached during the Republic's heyday. Lace-making was both a creative expression and a highly lucrative craft, although the skill was nearly lost several times as handmade lace went in and out of fashion. (Lace Museum; 041 73 00 34; www.museomerletto.visitmuve.it; Piazza Galuppi 185, Burano; adult/reduced €5/3.50, with Museum Pass free; 10am-5pm; Burano)

Borges Labyrinth

## Monastero di San Lazzaro degli Armeni MONASTERY

3 MAP P162, D4

Tours of this historic island monastery are usually conducted by its multilingual Armenian monks, who amply demonstrate the institution's reputation for scholarship. The St Lazarus Monastery is a fascinating repository of Armenian history, art and culture – and much more besides. Significant manuscripts from its 170,000-item library are on display, alongside curios from Ancient Egypt, Rome, Sumeria and India. (041 526 01 04; Isola di San Lazzaro degli Armeni; adult/reduced €6/4.50; tours 3.25pm; San Lazzaro)

### Regatta Revelry

The biggest event in the northern lagoon calendar is the 32km **Vogalonga long row** (www.vogalonga.com; May/Jun) from Venice to Murano and back each May. It's a fabulously festive occasion when hundreds of enthusiasts take to the waters in their wooden *batèla* (flat-bottomed boats) and motorised boats are banned from the lagoon for the day.

Plan in advance and find a grassy picnic spot on Mazzorbo. If you'd like to have a go yourself get in touch with **Row Venice** (p130).

## Cimitero di San Michele CEMETERY

4 MAP P162, D3

Until Napoleon established a city cemetery on this little island, Venetians had been buried in parish plots across town – not an ideal solution in a watery city. Today, goths, incorrigible romantics and music lovers pause here to pay respects to Ezra Pound, Joseph Brodsky, Sergei Diaghilev and Igor Stravinsky. Pick up a map from the office to the left of the entrance and join them, but be aware, the map pinpointing of the famous graves isn't accurate. (Isola di San Michele; admission free; 7.30am-6pm Apr-Sep, to 4.30pm Oct-Mar; Cimitero)

## Acquolina Cooking School COOKING

5 MAP P162, D4

These intimate cookery classes are held by Marika Contaldo in her flower-festooned Lido villa. Serious gourmets will want to consider the multiday culinary vacations, which include cookery lessons interspersed with market visits, lagoon cruises and trips to the Segusa glass factory. Otherwise, there are half- and full-day taster courses, the latter including a morning trip to the Rialto Market. (041 526 72 26; www.acquolina.com; Via Lazzaro Mocenigo 10, Lido; half-/full-day courses €170/290; ; Lido)

# Eating

## Trattoria Altanella VENETIAN €€

6 MAP P162, C4

Founded by fisherfolk in 1920 and still run by the same family, this cosy restaurant serves classic Venetian fare such as potato gnocchi with cuttlefish, stuffed squid and perfectly grilled fish. The vintage interior is hung with paintings, reflecting the restaurant's popularity with local artists, and there are also tables on a flower-fringed balcony jutting out over the canal. (041 522 77 80; Calle de le Erbe 268, Giudecca; meals €41-46; 12.30-2pm & 7.30-9pm Wed-Sun; ; Redentore)

## Locanda Cipriani VENETIAN €€€

7 MAP P162, F1

Run by the Cipriani family since 1935, the Locanda is Harry's Bar gone rustic, with a wood-beamed dining room opening onto a pretty garden. But standards are standards, so staff buzz about in dapper bow ties, theatrically silver serving every dish – even the pasta! The kitchen is just as precise, delivering pillowy gnocchi, perfectly cooked fish and decadent chocolate mousse. (041 73 01 50; www.locandacipriani.com; Piazza Torcello 29, Torcello; meals €54-69; noon-3pm Wed-Mon Mar-Dec, plus 6-11pm Fri & Sat Apr-Sep; Torcello)

### Boating on the Lagoon

**Terra e Acqua** (347 4205004; www.veneziainbarca.it; day trips from €400) offers wild rides to the outer edges of the lagoon on a sturdy motorised *bragozzo* (flat-bottomed fishing vessel) accommodating up to 12 people. Itineraries are customised, and can cover abandoned quarantine islands and the hard-to-reach friary on Isola di San Francesco del Deserto.

For those who like to be in charge of their own destiny, **Venice Kayak** (Map p162, E3; 346 4771327; www.venicekayak.com; Vento di Venezia, Isola della Certosa; half-/full-day tours €95/125) organises well-planned tours in the warren of Venice's canals and out to remote islands in the broad garden of the lagoon.

## Acquastanca VENETIAN €€€

8 MAP P162, D2

A modern sensibility imbues both the decor and the menu at this wonderful little restaurant. An array of old-fashioned Murano mirrors adorns a wall, while twigs hang artfully from the ceiling. Seafood features prominently on a menu that includes octopus with chickpeas and a panoply of pasta. (041 319 51 25; www.acquastanca.it; Fondamenta Manin 48, Murano; meals

### Venissa: A Mazzorbo Renaissance

In 1999, Gianluca Bisol, a *prosecco* producer from Valdobbiadene, heard of an ancient vineyard enclosed by medieval walls on Mazzorbo. He rented the land from the city and set about rehabilitating the rare Renaissance Dorona grape from just 88 vines which had survived.

Once he'd reclaimed the Venissa vineyard, he turned his attention to the farm buildings, which he converted into a contemporary six-room **guesthouse** and the **Venissa Osteria**. Since then a Michelin-starred **restaurant** (Map p162, F1; 041 527 22 81; www.venissa.it; Fondamenta Santa Caterina 3, Mazzorbo; set menu €110-175; 12.30-2pm & 7.30-9pm Wed-Mon Apr-Oct; Mazzorbo) has been added in the garden.

The entire Mazzorbo operation is now managed by Gianluca's son Matteo, and his latest project has been the opening of **Casa Burano** (p173), an *albergo diffuso* (multi-venue hotel) with 13 rooms spread through five cottages on Burano.

€48-54; 10am-4pm & 7-10pm Mon & Fri, 10am-4pm Tue-Thu & Sat, extended in summer; Faro)

## La Palanca VENETIAN **€€**

9 MAP P162, C3

Locals of all ages pour into this humble bar for *cicheti* (Venetian tapas), coffee and a *spritz* (prosecco cocktail). However, it's at lunchtime that it really comes into its own, serving surprisingly sophisticated fare like swordfish carpaccio with orange zest alongside more rustic dishes, such as a delicious *pasta e fagioli* (pasta and bean soup). In summer, competition for waterside tables is stiff. (041 528 77 19; www.facebook.com/LaPalancaGiudecca; Fondamenta Sant'Eufemia 448, Giudecca; meals €24-40; 7am-8.30pm Mon-Sat; ; Palanca)

## Venissa Osteria VENETIAN **€€€**

10 MAP P162, F1

A more affordable companion piece to its Michelin-starred sister, this upmarket *osteria* offers updates on Venetian classics such as marinated fish, duck tagliatelle and *bigoli* (thick wholemeal pasta with anchovies). For an extra treat, splash out on a glass of dorona, the prestigious golden-hued wine varietal only grown here. (041 527 22 81; www.venissa.it; Fondamenta Santa Caterina 3, Mazzorbo; meals €37-56; noon-4pm & 7-9pm daily Apr-Nov, Thu-Mon Dec-Mar; Mazzorbo)

### Favorita

VENETIAN **€€€**

11 MAP P162, E4

Favorita has been delivering long, lazy lunches, bottles of fine wine and impeccable service since 1955. The menu is full of traditional Venetian seafood dishes such as *rombo* (turbot) simmered with cherry tomatoes and olives, crab *gnochetti* (mini-gnocchi) and classic fish risotto. (041 526 16 26; Via Francesco Duodo 33, Lido; meals €41-55; 7-10.30pm Tue-Thu, 12.30-2.30pm & 7-10.30pm Fri-Sun; A)

### Osteria al Duomo

ITALIAN **€€**

12 MAP P162, D2

Opened in 1903 by the parish priest as a co-op grocery shop, this *osteria* (casual tavern) is still collectively owned by 50 Muranese families. Don't be surprised, then, by the friendly vibe, honest bowls of pasta (the swordfish, olive and tomato spaghetti is excellent) and some of the best pizza in Venice. In summer, sit out in the walled garden. (041 527 43 03; www.osteriaalduomo.com; Fondamenta Maschio 20-21, Murano; meals €23-46; 11am-10.30pm; ; Museo)

### Magiche Voglie

GELATO **€**

13 MAP P162, D4

The best ice cream on the Lido is made on the premises of this family-owned gelateria every morning. Decide between the soft peaks of New World flavours such as açai berry and caja fruit, or plump for the classic purplish-black cherry or Sicilian pistachio. (347 7943992; Gran Viale Santa Maria

Waterfront cafe on the Lido

### A Spa with a View

Set on a 16-hectare private island, 20 minutes from Piazza San Marco, JW Marriott's Venetian **hotel** (Map p162, C4; 041 852 13 00; www.jwvenice.com; Isola delle Rose; r/ste from €352/572; ) is a bucolic haven in the lagoon. While Matteo Thun's contemporary, minimalist interiors and rooms are elegant in the extreme, it's the **rooftop spa and pools** (indoor and outdoor), with their four-poster loungers and unimpeded views across the lagoon, that really steal the show.

Non-hotel guests can access the island via the free shuttle from San Marco Giardinetti. Even the basic package offering use of the facilities is worth the trip, otherwise there are a range of massages (€125 to €170), hammam treatments (€90) and even a Michelin-starred restaurant.

Elisabetta 47g, Lido; cones €2.50-4.50; 2.30-9pm Fri-Sun Mar & Oct, 10am-11pm Apr-Sep; Lido SME)

### Trattoria al Gatto Nero

VENETIAN **€€€**

14 MAP P162, F1

Don't expect fancy tricks from this 'Black Cat' – just excellent, traditional fare. Once you've tried the homemade *tagliolini* (ribbon pasta) with spider crab, whole grilled fish and perfect house-baked biscuits, the ferry ride to Burano seems a minor inconvenience – a swim back here from Venice would be worth it for the mixed seafood grill alone. Call ahead and plead for canalside seating. (041 73 01 20; www.gattonero.com; Fondamenta della Giudecca 88, Burano; meals €42-70; 12.30-3pm & 7.30-9pm Tue-Sun; Burano)

### Trattoria ai Cacciatori

VENETIAN **€€**

15 MAP P162, C3

If you hadn't guessed from the oversized gun hanging from the ceiling beams, the restaurant is named for the hunters who once bagged lagoon waterfowl. Dishes are hearty but sophisticated, including both game and local seafood. (328 7363346; www.aicacciatori.it; Fondamenta del Ponte Piccolo 320, Giudecca; meals €34-47; noon-3pm & 6.30-10pm Tue-Sun; ; Palanca)

## Drinking

### Skyline

ROOFTOP BAR

16 MAP P162, C3

From white-sneaker cruise passengers to the €300-sunglasses set, the rooftop bar at the Hilton Molino Stucky wows everyone with its vast panorama over Venice and the lagoon. DJs spin tunes on Friday nights year-round, and on additional nights in summer, when the action moves to the deck and pool. There's occasional live music too. (041 272 33 11; www.skylinebar-venice.it; Fondamenta San Biagio 810, Giudecca; noon-1am Apr-Oct, 4pm-midnight Nov-Mar; Palanca)

### Essentiale

BAR

17 MAP P162, D4

Sunset photo ops don't come any better than on the terrace of the Habsburg-era Villa Laguna, with views over San Marco framed by a blushing pink sky. While Essentiale is essentially a restaurant, it also caters to the *aperitivo* crowd. And it's very handy to the Lido SME ferry terminal. (041 526 13 16; www.essentialerestaurant.com; Via Sandro Gallo 6, Lido; 12.30pm-midnight Tue-Sun; Lido SME)

### Caffè-Bar Palmisano

CAFE

18 MAP P162, F1

Refuel with espresso and a toasted sandwich at this cafe on the sunny side of the street, and return later to celebrate photo-safari triumphs over *spritz* or wine with regular crowds of fisherfolk and university students. (Via Galuppi 351, Burano; 7am-9pm; Burano)

## Shopping

### Emilia

ARTS & CRAFTS

Doyenne Emilia di Ammendola, a third-generation lace-maker, has passed on her skills to her children who are continuing the family tradition in this flagship store (see 2 Map p162, F1); there's another on Calle San Mauro and a branch in Los Angeles. Prices befit the quality (ie out of this world), but you can take away a tiny souvenir for €10. There's a family museum upstairs. (041 73 52 99; www.emiliaburano.it; Via Galuppi 205, Burano; 9.30am-7pm; Burano)

### Fornace Mian

GLASS

19 MAP P162, D2

Shuffle past the typical Murano kitsch (glass pandas, parrots in trees etc) and you'll find one of the best ranges of classic stemware on the island. If there isn't enough of your favourite design in stock, it can be made to order and shipped internationally. (041 73 94 23; www.fornacemian.com; Fondamenta da Mula 143, Murano; 9.30am-5.30pm; Venier)

### Cartavenezia

ARTS & CRAFTS

20 MAP P162, C4

Paper is anything but two-dimensional here: paper maestro Fernando di Masone embosses and sculpts handmade cotton paper into seamless raw-edged lampshades, hand-bound sketchbooks, and paper versions of marble friezes that would seem equally at home in a Greek temple or a modern loft. White gloves are handy for easy, worry-free browsing; paper-sculpting courses are available by prior request. (041 524 12 83; www.cartavenezia.it; Campo San Cosmo 621f, Giudecca; by appointment; Palanca)

# Survival Guide



Basilica di Santa Maria della Salute (p72) CANADASTOCK/SHUTTERSTOCK ©

# Before You Go

## Book Your Stay

- Book ahead for weekend getaways and high-season visits.
- Although Venice is a small city, getting around it can be complicated, so plan where you stay carefully. Easy access to *a vaporetto* (small passenger ferry) stop is key.
- Check individual hotel websites for online deals.
- Confirm arrival at least 72 hours in advance, or hotels may assume you've changed plans.
- For low-season savings of 40% or more, plan visits for November, early December or January to March (except Carnevale). Deals may be found July to August.

### Venice

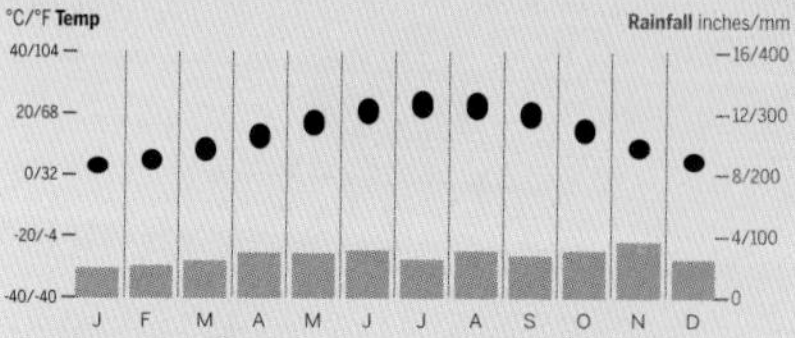


### When to Go

- **Spring (Mar–May)** Damp but lovely as ever indoors. Bring an umbrella and enjoy bargain rates – except at Easter.
- **Summer (Jun–Aug)** The Biennale draws the crowds. Temperatures rise and the Rialto is hot, crowded and expensive. Locals escape to the Lido.
- **Autumn (Sep–Nov)** After the Venice Film Festival, crowds retreat and rates drop, but the sun still shines.
- **Winter (Dec–Feb)** Chilly days with some fog, but nights are sociable, especially during Carnevale.

## Useful Websites

- **Luxrest Venice** (☎041 296 05 61; www.luxrest-venice.com; Ponte del Pistor 5990, Castello) Carefully curated, hand-picked selection of apartments.
- **Lonely Planet** (lonelyplanet.com/italy/venice/hotels) Expert author reviews, user feedback engine.
- **Venice Prestige** (www.veniceprestige.com) Venetian apartments to rent in aristocratic palaces in the best locations in town.
- **Views on Venice** (☎041 241 11 49; www.viewsonvenice.com) Apartments picked for their personality, character and view, of course.
- **Fairbnb Venice** (https://fairbnb.coop/venice) A community-powered home-sharing platform where 50% of booking fees support local projects.

## Best Budget

**Allo Squero** (☎041 523 69 73; www.allosquero.it; Corte dello Squero 4692; d €120; ; Fondamente Nove) Cannaregio home comforts.

**Le Terese** (☎041 523 17 28; www.leterese.com; Campiello Tron

1902; r €100; ; Santa Marta) A home from home with two architect-styled rooms.

**Albergo San Samuele** ( 041 520 51 65; www.hotelsansamuele.com; Salizada San Samuele 3358; d €140-175, s/d without bathroom €96/105; ; San Samuele) Rock-bottom prices right by Palazzo Grassi.

**Generator** ( 041 877 82 88; www.generatorhostels.com; Fondamenta de la Croce 86, Giudecca; dm/r from €36/153; ; Zitelle) Contemporary hostel cool with canal views.

## Best Midrange

**Locanda Ca' Le Vele** ( 041 241 39 60; www.locandalevele.com; Calle de le Vele 3969; d €122-148, ste €165-183; ; Ca' d'Oro) Boutique B&B with a heavy dose of Venetian glam.

**Venice Halldis Apartments** ( 02 8929 3558; www.halldis.com; Calle Priuli dei Cavalletti 96t; apt from €189; ; Ferrovia) Light, bright, well-priced, Scandi-style modern apartments.

**Oltre Il Giardino** ( 041 275 00 15; www.oltreilgiardino-venezia.com; Fondamenta Contarini 2542; d/ste from €180/280; ; San Tomà) A romantic garden retreat once home to Alma Mahler's widow.

**Residenza de L'Osmarin** ( 347 4501440; www.residenzadelosmarin.com; Calle Rota 4960; d €170-250; ; San Zaccaria) A true B&B with quilted bedspreads and a slap-up breakfast.

**Casa Burano** ( 041 527 22 81; www.casaburano.it; Burano; r/ste from €108/144; ) Pastel-coloured cottages full of locally crafted furnishings.

## Best Top End

**Gritti Palace** ( 041 79 46 11; www.thegrittipalace.com; Campo di Santa Maria del Giglio 2467; r from €874; ; Giglio) Grand Canal rooms in a doge's palace.

**Al Ponte Antico** ( 041 241 19 44; www.alponteantico.com; Calle de l'Aseo 5768; d €330; ; Rialto) Old-world glamour accompanied by gracious service.

**Hotel Palazzo Barbarigo** ( 041 74 01 72; www.palazzobarbarigo.com; Calle Corner 2765; r/ste from €252/351; ; San Tomà) Seductive rooms handily supplied with fainting couches.

**Palazzo Abadessa** ( 041 241 37 84; www.abadessa.com; Calle Priuli 4011; r €225-335; ; Ca' d'Oro) Frescoed rooms, canal views and a lily-scented garden.

# Arriving in Venice

## Marco Polo Airport

**Marco Polo Airport** ( flight information 041 260 92 60; www.veniceairport.it; Via Galileo Gallilei 30/1, Tessera) is Venice's main international airport and is located in Tessera, 12km east of Mestre.

Inside the terminal you'll find ticket offices for water taxis and Alilaguna water bus transfers, an ATM, currency exchange offices, a **left-luggage office** (Marco Polo Airport, Tessera; first 6hr per item €6, thereafter per hr €0.30, bikes per 24hr

€14; 5am-9pm) and a Vènezia Unica **tourist office** (041 24 24; www.veneziaunica.it; Arrivals Hall, Marco Polo Airport; 8.30am-7pm) where you can pick up pre-ordered travel cards and a map.

## Alilaguna Airport Shuttle

**Alilaguna** (041 240 17 01; www.alilaguna.it; airport transfer one-way €15) operates four water shuttles that link the airport with various parts of Venice at a cost of €8 to Murano and €15 to all other landing stages. The ride takes 45 to 90 minutes to reach most destinations. Lines include the following:

**Linea Blu** (Blue Line) Stops at Lido, San Marco and Dorsoduro.

**Linea Rossa** (Red Line) Stops at Murano and Lido.

**Linea Arancia** (Orange Line) Stops at Stazione VeneziaSanta Lucia, Rialto and San Marco via the Grand Canal.

**Linea Gialla** (Yellow Line) Stops at Murano and Fondamente Nove (Cannaregio).

## Bus

Piazzale Roma is the only point within central Venice accessible by bus. *Vaporetto* lines and water taxis depart from Piazzale Roma docks.

- **ACTV** (Azienda del Consorzio Trasporti Veneziano; 041 272 2111; http://actv.avmspa.it/en) Bus 5 runs between Marco Polo Airport and Piazzale Roma (€8, 30 minutes, four per hour). A bus+single *vaporetto* ticket costs €14.
- **ATVO** (0421 59 46 71; www.atvo.it; Piazzale Roma 497g; 6.40am-7.30pm; Piazzale Roma) Buses depart from the airport to **Piazzale Roma** (€8, 25 minutes, every 30 minutes from 8am to midnight).

## Water Taxi

- Water taxis can be booked at the **Consorzio Motoscafi Venezia** (041 240 67 12; www.motoscafivenezia.it; 9am-6pm Mon-Fri) or **Venezia Taxi** (info 328 2389661; www.veneziataxi.it) desks in the arrivals hall, or directly at the dock. Private taxis cost from €110 for up to four passengers and all their luggage.
- A shared taxi costs from €25 per person with a €6 surcharge for night-time arrivals. Seats should be booked online at www.venicelink.com. Be aware that shared taxis can wait some time to fill up and have set drop-off points in Venice.
- Boats seat a maximum of eight people and accommodate up to 10 bags.

## Taxi

A taxi from the aiport to Piazzale Roma costs €50. From there you can either hop on a *vaporetto* or pick up a **water taxi** (Fondamente Cossetti) at Fondamente Cossetti.

## Car

- Cars cannot be taken into central Venice. At Piazzale Roma and Tronchetto parking garages expect to pay from €15 per day.
- From Piazzale Roma docks, you can take a *vaporetto* or water taxi.
- A **monorail** (www.avmspa.it; Piazzale Roma; per ride €1.50; 7.10am-10.50pm Mon-Sat, 8.40am-8.50pm Sun), also known

as the People Mover, connects the Tronchetto parking lots to Piazzale Roma (€1.50 per person).

## Stazione Venezia Santa Lucia

All mainland trains terminate in Venice's **Santa Lucia train station** (www.veneziasantalucia.it; Fondamenta Santa Lucia), appearing on signs as Ferrovia within Venice. The station has a helpful **tourist office** (041 24 24; www.veneziaunica.it; 7am-9pm; Ferrovia) opposite platform 3 where you can obtain a map and buy *vaporetto* tickets, and a **left-luggage depot** (Left Luggage Office; 041 78 55 31; Stazione Venezia Santa Lucia; 6am-11pm) opposite platform 1.

### Vaporetto

*Vaporetti* connect Santa Lucia train station with all parts of Venice. Lines include the following:

**Line 1** Covers the Grand Canal to San Marco and the Lido every 10 minutes.

**Line 2** Covers the Grand Canal with fewer stops, returning via Giudecca.

**Lines 4.1 & 4.2** Circles Venice's outer perimeter. Convenient for Cannaregio and Castello.

**Lines 5.1 & 5.2** Covers the 4.1 and 4.2 route, plus the Lido, with fewer stops..

**Line N** All-night service stops along Giudecca, the Grand Canal, San Marco and the Lido.

### Water Taxi

The water taxi stand is outside the station on Fondamente Cossetti; fares start at €15 and add up quickly at €2 per minute.

# Getting Around

### Vaporetto

- The city's main mode of public transport is the *vaporetto* (small passenger ferry).
- **ACTV** (Azienda del Consorzio Trasporti Veneziano; 041 272 2111; http://actv.avmspa.it/en) runs all public transport in Venice, including all the waterborne public transport.
- Major stops often have two separate docks serving the same *vaporetto* line, heading in opposite directions. Check landing dock signs to make sure you're at the right dock for the direction you want.
- Main lines get full fast, especially between 8am to 10am and 6pm to 8pm. Also, boats can be overcrowded during Carnevale and in peak season.
- Line N offers all-night local service covering Giudecca, the Grand Canal, San Marco and the Lido (11.30am to 4am, about every 40 minutes).
- Inter-island ferry services to Murano, Torcello, the Lido and other lagoon islands are usually provided on larger *motonave* (big inter-island *vaporetti*).

### Tickets & Passes

- **Vènezia Unica** (041 24 24; www.veneziaunica.it) is the main ticket seller, and you can purchase *vaporetti* tickets at booths at most landing stations. Tickets and multiday passes can also be pre-purchased online.

- A one-way tickets cost €7.50.
- If you're going to be using the *vaporetto* frequently (more than three trips), consider a Travel Card, which allows unlimited travel in set time periods.
- Always validate your ticket at yellow dockside machines at first usage. If you're caught without a valid ticket you'll be fined €59 (plus the €7.50 fare) on the spot.
- People aged 14 to 29 holding a Rolling Venice card (p179) can get a three-day ticket for €20 at tourist offices.

## Gondola

- Rates are €80 for 40 minutes (it's €100 for 35 minutes from 7pm to 8am), not including songs or tips. Additional time is charged in 20-minute increments (day/night €40/50).
- Gondolas cluster at *stazi* (stops) along the Grand Canal and near major monuments and tourist hot spots, but you can also book a pick-up by calling **Ente Gondola** (041 528 50 75; www.gondolavenezia.it).
- **Gondolas 4 All** (328 2431382; www.gondolas4all.com; Fondamente Cossetti; per 30min €80; Piazzale Roma), supported by the Gondoliers Association, offers gondola rides to wheelchair users in a specially adapted gondola. Embarkation is from a wheelchair-accessible pier at Piazzale Roma.

## Traghetto

A *traghetto* is the gondola service locals use to cross the Grand Canal between bridges (€2, 9am to 6pm, some routes to noon).

## Water Taxi

- Licensed water taxis offer stylish transport in sleek teak boats.
- Fares start at €15 plus €2 per minute, €5 extra if they're called to your hotel. There's a €10 surcharge for night trips (10pm to 6am), a €5 surcharge for additional luggage (above five pieces) and a €10 surcharge for each extra passenger above the first four. Tipping isn't required.
- If you order a water taxi through your hotel or a travel agent, you will be subject to a surcharge.
- Even if you're in a hurry, don't encourage your taxi driver to speed – *motoschiaffi* (motorboat wakes) expose Venice's ancient foundations to degradation.

## Bicycle

- Cycling is banned in central Venice.
- On the Lido, cycling is a pleasant way to reach distant beaches.
- **Lido on Bike** (041 526 80 19; www.lidoonbike.it; Gran Viale Santa Maria Elisabetta 21b, Lido; bicycle rental per 90min/day €5/10; 9am-7pm summer; Lido SME) is located near the *vaporetto* (small passenger ferry) stop; ID is required for rental.

# Essential Information

## Accessible Travel

With nearly 400 footbridges and endless stairs, Venice is not an easy place for travellers with disabilities.

- *Vaporetti* are the most effective way to access sites and avoid bridges. Passengers in wheelchairs travel for just €1.50, while their companion travels free.
- The **Disabled Assistance Office** (Sala Blu; ☎800 906 060; Stazione Venezia Santa Lucia; ⏰6.45am-9.30pm) is located at platform 4 in Venice's Santa Lucia train station.
- The most accessible tourist office is the one off Piazza San Marco.
- With ID, most museums offer free or discounted admission to disabled visitors with one companion.
- A printable *Accessible Venice* map is available from the tourist office. The map delimits the area around each water-bus stop that can be accessed without crossing a bridge. In addition, the website provides 12 'barrier-free' itineraries, which can be downloaded.
- Of the other islands, Murano, Burano, the Lido and Torcello are all fairly easy to access.

Download Lonely Planet's free Accessible Travel guide from http://lptravel.to/AccessibleTravel.

## Organisations

**Gondolas 4 All** (☎328 2431382; www.gondolas4all.com; Fondamente Cossetti; per 30min €80; ⛴Piazzale Roma) Manual (not electric) wheelchair users can now experience the city's iconic mode of transport. It's advisable to use the booking form on their Italian-language website.

**L'Altra Venezia** (www.laltravenezia.it; walking tours per hour €70, thematic tours from €200, boat tours from €400) Offers half- and full-day city and lagoon tours in specially adapted boats that can accommodate up to seven people (maximum four wheelchairs). Tours are proposed 'pilot only' or with a guide, and include lunch on-board or in local restaurants.

**Rome & Italy** (☎06 4425 8441; www.romeanditaly.com/tourism-for-disabled; Via Giuseppe Veronese 50; ⏰9am-8pm) is a mainstream travel agency with an accessible tourism arm that offers two, half-day customised tours in Venice to the Doge's palace and Torcello island, accessible accommodation, and equipment and vehicle hire.

**Accessible Italy** (www.accessibleitaly.com) is a San Marino–based nonprofit company that specialises in holiday services for people with disabilities, including equipment rental, adapted vehicle hire and arranging personal assistants. In Venice, they offer multiday individual, group and bespoke tours.

**Sage Traveling** (www.sagetraveling.com), a US-based accessible-travel agency, offering tailor-made tours in Europe. Check out their website for a detailed access guide to Venice, which includes tips on how to use the *vaporetto* and water taxis, accessible walking and boating tours, and hotels.

## Business Hours

The hours listed here are a general guide; individual establishments can vary.

## Dos & Don'ts

- Do keep right along narrow lanes and let people pass on the left.
- Don't linger on small bridges taking photographs at lunchtime and 3pm during the school run. And, avoid selfie sticks which threaten to poke passers-by in the eye.
- Do offer help to people struggling with strollers or bags on bridges.
- Don't push. Allow passengers to disembark before boarding boats. Pay attention to calls of *'Permesso!'* (Pardon!) as people try to exit busy boats.

**Banks** 8.30am to 1.30pm and 3.30pm to 5.30pm Monday to Friday; some open Saturday mornings.

**Restaurants** Noon to 2.30pm and 7pm to 10pm.

**Shops** 10am to 1pm and 3.30pm to 7pm (or 4pm to 7.30pm) Monday to Saturday.

## Discount Cards

The tourist information portal, **Vènezia Unica** (☎041 24 24; www.veneziaunica.it), brings together a range of discount passes and services and enables you to tailor them to your needs and pre-purchase online. Services and passes on offer include the following:

- land and water transfers to the airport and cruise terminal
- ACTV Travel Cards
- museum and church passes
- select parking
- citywide wi-fi
- prepaid access to public toilets

If purchasing online you need to print out your voucher displaying your reservation number (PNR) and carry it with you, then simply present it at the various attractions for admission/access.

To use public transport, you will need to obtain a free card (you will need your PNR code to do this), which is then 'loaded' with credit. Get this at the ACTV ticket machines at Marco Polo Airport, ticket desks at *vaporetto* stops and Vènezia Unica offices.

### Chorus Pass

Offers single entry to 16 churches (adult/student under 29 years €12/8). Valid for one year. Buy at participating churches.

### Civic Museum Pass

This pass (adult/reduced €24/18) is valid for six months and covers single entry to 11 civic museums, including Palazzo Ducale and the Museo Correr. Available from any civic museum or the tourist office.

### City Pass

City passes are available from Vènezia Unica. The most useful:

**City Pass** (adult/junior €39.90/29.90) Valid for seven days, offering entrance to 11 civic museums, 16 Chorus churches, the Fondazione Querini Stampalia and the Museo Ebraico

(Jewish Museum). It also includes free admission to the casino.

**St Mark's City Pass** (€27.90) A reduced version of the City Pass allowing entry to the three civic museums on Piazza San Marco, plus three churches on the Chorus Circuit and the Fondazione Querini Stampalia.

## Other Combined Museum Tickets

- A combined ticket to Ca' d'Oro and Palazzo Grimani costs adult/student/senior €10/8/free and is valid for three months.
- A combined ticket to the Palazzo Grassi and Punta della Dogana costs adult/reduced €18/15.

## Rolling Venice Card

Visitors aged six to 29 years should pick up the €6 Rolling Venice card (from tourist offices and most ACTV public transport ticket points), entitling purchase of a 72-hour public transport pass (€22) and discounts on airport transfers, museums, monuments and cultural events.

## Electricity

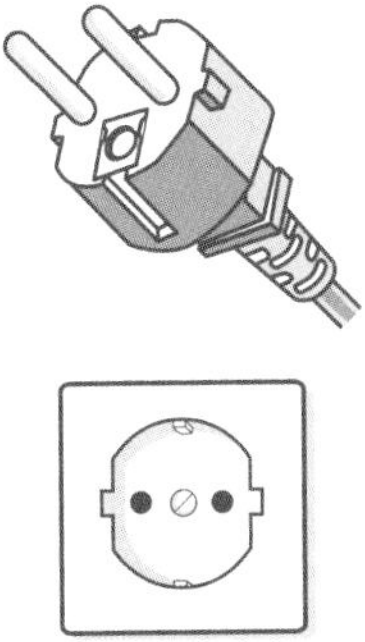

**Type F**
**230V/50Hz**

**Type L**
**220V/50Hz**

## Money

**ATMs** Widely available

**Credit cards** Accepted at most hotels, B&Bs and shops.

**Money changers** At banks, airport and some hotels; you'll need ID.

**Tipping** Ten per cent optional for good restaurant, hotel and gondola services.

## Public Holidays

Holidays that may affect opening hours and transit schedules:

**Capodanno/Anno Nuovo** (New Year's Day) 1 January

**Epifania/Befana** (Epiphany) 6 January

**Pasquetta/Lunedì dell'Angelo** (Easter Monday) March/April

**Giorno della Liberazione** (Liberation Day) 25 April

**Festa del Lavoro** (Labour Day) 1 May

**Festa della Repubblica** (Republic Day) 2 June

**Ferragosto** (Feast of the Assumption) 15 August

**Ognissanti** (All Saints' Day) 1 November

**Immaculata Concezione** (Feast of the Immaculate Conception) 8 December

**Natale** (Christmas Day) 25 December

**Festa di Santo Stefano** (Boxing Day) 26 December

## Safe Travel

**Precautions** Mind your step on slippery canal banks, especially after rains. Watch out for petty theft around Venice's train station.

**Children** Few canal banks and bridges have railings, and most Gothic palaces have lots of stairs.

**Rising water** Flooding in low-lying areas is a regular occurrence in Venice.

## Telephone

### Mobile Phones

GSM and tri-band phones can be used in Italy with a local SIM card.

### Phone Codes

Italy's country code is ☎39. The city code for Venice is ☎041. The city code is an integral part of the number and must always be dialled. Toll-free (freephone) numbers are known as *numeri verdi* and usually start with 800.

### International Calls

The cheapest options for calling internationally are free or low-cost computer programs such as Skype, FaceTime and Viber, cut-rate call centres or international dialling cards, which are sold at news-stands and tobacconists.

If you're calling an international number from an Italian phone, you must dial 00 to get an international line, then the relevant country and city codes, followed by the telephone number.

To call Venice from abroad, call the international access number for Italy (011 in the United States, 00 from most other countries), Italy's country code ☎39, then the Venice area code ☎041, followed by the telephone number.

## Toilets

**Public toilets** Available near tourist attractions (€1.50) and open from 7am to 7pm.

**Bars and cafes** For customers only. Look before you sit: even in women's bathrooms, some toilets don't have seats.

**Museums** This is your best option – where available.

## Tourist Information

- **Vènezia Unica** (☎041 24 24; www.veneziaunica.it) runs all tourist information services and offices in Venice. It provides information on sights, itineraries, day trips, transport, special events, shows and temporary exhibitions. Discount passes can be prebooked on its website.
- Find offices at Marco Polo Airport, Santa Lucia train station and on Piazza San Marco.

## Visas

Not required for EU citizens. Nationals of Australia, Brazil, Canada,

Japan, New Zealand, the UK and the USA do not need visas for visits of up to 90 days. For more information, visit the Italian foreign ministry website (www.esteri.it).

## Covid Travel Requirements

All passengers entering Italy must fill in a digital European Passenger Locator Form (PLF). In addition:

- People travelling from the EU and Schengen countries must show a Green Pass (vaccination certificate) or proof of a negative molecular swab test completed within 48 hours of entering Italy.
- People travelling from the UK must show a Green Pass (or equivalent certificate) and a negative test result from within 48 hours of entry.
- People travelling from Canada, the US, or Japan must show a Green Pass (or equivalent certificate) and a negative test result from within 72 hours of entry.
- For further details see www.esteri.it.

# Responsible Travel

## COVID-19 Protocols

- Under Italy's current COVID-19 regulations, you're required to wear a mask to access indoor tables at restaurants and to enter churches, museums, cultural sites etc.
- Regulations can change at short notice – check the latest at www.italia.it/en/useful-info/covid-19-updates-information-for-tourists.html

## Overtourism

- Time your stay: avoid the worst crowds by visiting in autumn (Oct-Nov) or winter (Jan-Feb). Midweek is quieter than weekends.
- Venture out of the centre: explore *sestieri* such as Castello and Cannaregio and lagoon islands like Torcello.
- Overnight rather than day trip: check www.fairbnb.coop for community-minded rental accommodation.

## Support Local

- Take a tour with a local: try **Best Venice Guides** (http://bestveniceguides.it; per hr €65-85).
- Buy local: **Venezia Autentica** (https://veneziaautentica.com) lists shops, restaurants and bars that contribute to a sustainable local economy.

# Language

Regional dialects are an important part of identity in many parts of Italy, but you'll have no trouble being understood in Venice or anywhere else in the country if you stick to standard Italian, which is what we've also used in this chapter.

The sounds used in Italian can all be found in English. If you read our pronunciation guides as if they were English, you'll be understood. The stressed syllables are indicated with italics. Note that *ai* is pronounced as in 'aisle', *ay* as in 'say', *ow* as in 'how', *dz* as the 'ds' in 'lids', and that *r* is a strong and rolled sound.

To enhance your trip with a phrasebook, visit lonelyplanet.com.

## Basics

**Hello.**
*Buongiorno.* bwon·*jor*·no

**Goodbye.**
*Arrivederci.* a·ree·ve·*der*·chee

**How are you?**
*Come sta?* *ko*·me sta

**Fine. And you?**
*Bene. E Lei?* *be*·ne e lay

**Please.**
*Per favore.* per fa·*vo*·re

**Thank you.**
*Grazie.* *gra*·tsye

**Excuse me.**
*Mi scusi.* mee *skoo*·zee

**Sorry.**
*Mi dispiace.* mee dees·*pya*·che

**Yes./No.**
*Sì./No.* see/no

**I don't understand.**
*Non capisco.* non ka·*pee*·sko

**Do you speak English?**
*Parla inglese?* *par*·la een·*gle*·ze

## Eating & Drinking

| | | |
|---|---|---|
| **I'd like ...** | *Vorrei ...* | vo·*ray* .. |
| **a coffee** | *un caffè* | oon ka·*fe* |
| **a table** | *un tavolo* | oon *ta*·vo·lo |
| **the menu** | *il menù* | eel me·*noo* |
| **two beers** | *due birre* | doo·e *bee*·re |

**What would you recommend?**
*Cosa mi consiglia?* ko·za mee kon·*see*·lya

**Enjoy the meal!**
*Buon appetito!* bwon a·pe·*tee*·to

**That was delicious!**
*Era squisito!* e·ra skwee·zee·to

**Cheers!**
*Salute!* sa·*loo*·te

**Please bring the bill.**
*Mi porta il conto, per favore?* mee *por*·ta eel *kon* to per fa·*vo*·re

## Shopping

**I'd like to buy ...**
*Vorrei comprare ...* vo·*ray* kom·*pra*·re ...

**I'm just looking.**
*Sto solo guardando.* sto *so*·lo gwar·*dan*·do

**How much is this?**

| | |
|---|---|
| *Quanto costa questo?* | kwan·to kos·ta kwe·sto |

**It's too expensive.**

| | |
|---|---|
| *È troppo caro/ cara.* (m/f) | e tro·po ka·ro/ ka·ra |

## Emergencies

**Help!**

| | |
|---|---|
| *Aiuto!* | a·yoo·to |

**Call the police!**

| | |
|---|---|
| *Chiami la polizia!* | kya·mee la po·lee·tsee·a |

**Call a doctor!**

| | |
|---|---|
| *Chiami un medico!* | kya·mee oon me·dee·ko |

**I'm sick.**

| | |
|---|---|
| *Mi sento male.* | mee sen·to ma·le |

**I'm lost.**

| | |
|---|---|
| *Mi sono perso/ persa.* (m/f) | mee so·no per·so/ per·sa |

**Where are the toilets?**

| | |
|---|---|
| *Dove sono i gabinetti?* | do·ve so·no ee ga·bee·ne·tee |

## Time & Numbers

**What time is it?**

| | |
|---|---|
| *Che ora è?* | ke o·ra e |

**It's (two) o'clock.**

| | |
|---|---|
| *Sono le (due).* | so·no le (doo·e) |

| | | |
|---|---|---|
| **morning** | *mattina* | ma·tee·na |
| **afternoon** | *pomeriggio* | po·me·ree·jo |
| **evening** | *sera* | se·ra |
| **yesterday** | *ieri* | ye·ree |
| **today** | *oggi* | o·jee |
| **tomorrow** | *domani* | do·ma·nee |

| | | |
|---|---|---|
| **1** | *uno* | oo·no |
| **2** | *due* | doo·e |
| **3** | *tre* | tre |
| **4** | *quattro* | kwa·tro |
| **5** | *cinque* | cheen·kwe |
| **6** | *sei* | say |
| **7** | *sette* | se·te |
| **8** | *otto* | o·to |
| **9** | *nove* | no·ve |
| **10** | *dieci* | dye·chee |
| **100** | *cento* | chen·to |
| **1000** | *mille* | mee·le |

## Transport & Directions

**Where's ...?**

| | |
|---|---|
| *Dov'è ...?* | do·ve ... |

**What's the address?**

| | |
|---|---|
| *Qual'è l'indirizzo?* | kwa·le leen·dee·ree·tso |

**Can you show me (on the map)?**

| | |
|---|---|
| *Può mostrarmi (sulla pianta)?* | pwo mos·trar·mee (soo·la pyan·ta) |

**At what time does the ... leave?**

| | |
|---|---|
| *A che ora parte ...?* | a ke o·ra par·te |

**Does it stop at ...?**

| | |
|---|---|
| *Si ferma a ...?* | see fer·ma a ... |

**How do I get there?**

| | |
|---|---|
| *Come ci si arriva?* | ko·me chee see a·ree·va |

| | | |
|---|---|---|
| **bus** | *l'autobus* | low·to·boos |
| **ticket** | *un biglietto* | oon bee·lye·to |
| **timetable** | *orario* | o·ra·ryo |
| **train** | *il treno* | eel tre·no |

# Behind the Scenes

## Send Us Your Feedback

We love to hear from travellers – your comments help make our books better. We read every word, and we guarantee that your feedback goes straight to the authors. Visit **lonelyplanet.com/contact** to submit your updates and suggestions.

Note: We may edit, reproduce and incorporate your comments in Lonely Planet products such as guidebooks, websites and digital products, so let us know if you don't want your comments reproduced or your name acknowledged. For a copy of our privacy policy visit lonelyplanet.com/privacy.

## Paula's Thanks

*Grazie mille* to all the fun and fashionable Venetians who spilled the beans on their remarkable city: Paola dalla Valentina, Costanza Cecchini, Sara Porro, Lucia Cattaneo, Monica Cesarato, Francesca Giubilei, Luca Berta, Marco Secchi and Nan McElroy. Much love to Rob for sharing the beauty of the *bel paese.*

## Peter's Thanks

It turns out that it's not hard to find willing volunteers to keep you company on an extended research assignment in Venice, especially when it coincides with Carnevale. Many thanks to my Venice crew of Christine Henderson, Hamish Blennerhassett and Sarah Welch for much masked fun and many good meals. Special thanks to Christine for the translation services.

## Acknowledgements

Cover photographs: (front) Venice Carnevale. Koby Dagan / Shutterstock ©; (back) Murano glass manufacturing. Ldm Images / Shutterstock ©

## This Book

This 5th edition of Lonely Planet's *Pocket Venice* guidebook was researched and written by Paula Hardy, Peter Dragicevich and Duncan Garwood. The previous two editions were written by Alison Bing. This guidebook was produced by the following:

**Destination Editor** Anna Tyler

**Senior Product Editor** Daniel Bolger

**Product Editors** Paul Harding, Vicky Smith, Anne Mason

**Regional Senior Cartographer** Anthony Phelan

**Book Designers** Norma Prause-Brewer, Clara Monitto

**Assisting Editors** Gabby Innes, Monique Perrin, Kirsten Rawlings, Gabrielle Stefanos, Fionn Twomey

**Cartographers** Julie Dodkins, Valentina Kremenchutskaya

**Cover Researcher** Katherine Marsh

**Thanks to** Sasha Drew, Bruce Evans, Sonia Kapoor, Kate Mathews

# Index

See also separate subindexes for:

Eating p188
Drinking p189
Entertainment p189
Shopping p190



**Sights 000**
Map Pages **000**

**Sights 000**
Map Pages **000**

Index

**Sights 000**
Map Pages **000**

## Eating

## Shopping

# Our Writers

## Paula Hardy

Paula Hardy is an independent travel writer and editorial consultant, whose work for Lonely Planet and other flagship publications has taken her from nomadic camps in the Danakil Depression to Seychellois beach huts and the jewel-like bar at the Gritti Palace on the Grand Canal. Get in touch at www.paulahardy.com.

## Peter Dragicevich

After a successful career in niche newspaper and magazine publishing, both in his native New Zealand and in Australia, Peter finally gave into Kiwi wanderlust, giving up staff jobs to chase his diverse roots around much of Europe. Over the last decade he's written literally dozens of guidebooks for Lonely Planet on an oddly disparate collection of countries, all of which he's come to love.

## Duncan Garwood

From facing fast bowlers in Barbados to sidestepping hungry pigs in Goa, Duncan's travels have thrown up many unique experiences. These days he largely dedicates himself to Spain and Italy, his adopted homeland where he's been living since 1997.

**Published by Lonely Planet Global Limited**
CRN 554153
5th edition – Mar 2022
ISBN 978 1 78701 7580

10 9 8 7 6 5 4 3 2 1
Printed in Malaysia